The Glorious M5

Julian Phillips

Safe + enjoyable travels
on the M5 and beyond!

JAC Phillips

Published by New Generation Publishing in 2020

First Edition

ISBN

| | Paperback | 978-1-80031-509-9 |
| | Ebook | 978-1-80031-508-2 |

www.newgeneration-publishing.com

New Generation Publishing

The Glorious M5

Introduction from the author, Julian Phillips

A motorway is not just a fast road from A to B, it is a conduit between communities and points in time. It is a fast route to places of beauty and intrigue.

I was born and grew up in a family that runs a business operating coach tours. I spent many days, and sometimes weeks of my childhood touring the UK and Europe. Whilst it may not have been apparent to me as a youngster, I now appreciate the adage "travel broadens the mind". I now work in the very same family business and it is my job to research destinations and give our customers a commentary throughout the journey.

This short book is a written example of such a commentary. The M5 is the closest motorway to my hometown of Kidderminster. It is no exaggeration to say it is a motorway that I have driven the length of hundreds of times. The M5 has many stories to tell its travellers and many sights to show them – both natural and human-made. The M5 is glorious.

The M6 Interchange:

The first two miles of the M5 are between the M6 at Ray Hall and Junction 1 at West Bromwich. The completion of this section in May 1970 meant that there was continuous motorway between Ross-on-Wye in Herefordshire and Carnforth in Lancashire. At 192 miles, this was the longest continuous stretch of British motorway that could be driven at the time.

The first watercourse crossed by the M5 is the River Tame, a tributary of the River Trent. This is significant because the Tame is the only river crossed by the M5 that flows east of the English watershed, into the North Sea.

To the west of this section of motorway is Sandwell Valley Country Park, a 660-acre open space that used to be a Priory inhabited by Benedictine Monks until 1525. Maintained by the Local Authority, it offers a pleasant retreat from the urban areas of the Black Country and Birmingham and features numerous walking and cycling trails, sporting areas such as tennis courts and a swan pool. There are also two working farms in the Sandwell Valley, receiving parties of school children for educational tours, and three Golf Clubs.

The Hawthorns

Junction 1: West Bromwich

Junction 1 takes motorists into the heart of the Black Country, the epicentre of British industry for three centuries. The name 'Black Country' comes from the plumes of smoke that were emitted from the countless factories, mills, forges and steam locomotives that were the economic lifeblood of the region. It is said that Queen Victoria used to order the curtains closed on the Royal Train when it journeyed through the region to avoid the sight of sprawling industry.

One thing that is almost synonymous with industrial areas is football. The Black Country has three clubs in the English Football League: Walsall, Wolverhampton Wonderers and West Bromwich Albion. The latter, being closest to Junction 1, is based at The Hawthorns and is the highest league ground in England – 551 feet above sea level. West Bromwich Albion can be referred to as 'West Brom', the 'Albion' or the 'Baggies' – a nickname that is the subject of debate as to its origins.

Founded in 1878 and initially named "West Bromwich Strollers" because the original players had to walk 3 miles to buy a football, the Albion is a founding member of the football league. It has won the league once, the FA Cup five times and the League Cup once. It also remains the only team to obtain promotion and win the FA Cup in the same season: 1931. The club also played an important role in social history when it was the first team to field three black players in the late 1970s: Brendan Batson, Laurie Cunningham and Cyrille Regis. A statue of the trio can be seen outside the East stand at the Hawthorns.

The suffix 'wich' derives from an old English word 'wyche' and suggests that the area may have had a salt mine at one time. This is particularly the case further north in Cheshire where the towns of Northwich, Nantwich and Middlewich were a hub of salt mines for the Roman Empire.

Black Country Museum

Junctions 1 to 2: Overlooking the Black Country

The Oldbury viaduct is a lengthened 'fly-over' that stretches just over two miles between Junctions 1 and 2. Work began in 1967 and it opened in May 1970. A flyover was needed in this area because of the complex nature of the local road network. All other flyovers along the M5 were built to cross water.

An example of the complex nature of the road network around Oldbury is the main road between Birmingham and Wolverhampton (A4123) that passes under the M5 very close to Junction 2. An unusual interchange had to be constructed for Junction 2 due to an electricity substation being in close proximity with a junction between the A4123 and A4034 (Blackheath-West Bromwich Road). Removing the electricity substation was cost-prohibitive and so the slip roads of Junction 2 feed into a complex of two roundabouts from which the A4123 and A4034 now radiate. The new roundabout on the A4123 was the first in Britain to feature a right-hand turn, to allow utility vehicles to enter the electricity substation.

To enable construction, 120 homes and 55 industrial premises were either compulsorily purchased by the Ministry of Transport or altered by the works. 2,500 feet of the Birmingham Canal also had to be diverted. During the works, a pair of semi-detached houses on Penncricket Lane, Blackheath, were close to the new motorway cutting between Junctions 2 and 3. They were reconfigured so that the eastern house was completely demolished and the western property was re-designated as detached. The house survives today. The Oldbury Viaduct can support the passage of vehicles of up to 180 tonnes in weight, but regular observation and maintenance is needed. Long-term maintenance and upgrading of the flyover took place between 2016 and 2020.

The view stretches for miles on both sides. Looking west, motorists can see Turners Hill Radio and Television Transmitter. Behind Turners Hill is the traditional Black Country Town of Dudley. In its heyday Dudley's wealth stemmed from the local coal mines that provided the fuel to drive the area's factories, forges and mills and latterly the steam locomotives that carried goods from them all. Until the 1970s, Dudley was also one of the finest shopping centres in the Midlands, hosting many of the well-known chain stores and the department store Beatties.

The decline in Britain's coal and steel industry during the 1980s was a double whammy for Dudley. Mass redundancies for Dudley's labourers is something that the town is still recovering from to this day. The second 'whammy' was the closure of Round Oak Steel Works in nearby Brierley Hill. The Westfield 'Merry Hill' Centre was built on its site. An American style 'shopping mall' with dozens of shops and restaurants all under one roof and free car parking. Very quickly the chain stores that were the jewel in Dudley's crown moved to the Merry Hill Centre leaving several gaping holes in the town centre that are sadly evident in the 2020s.

Dudley still has a great deal to offer though. Its castle proudly overlooks the region despite being intentionally ruined during the Civil War because it was used as a base for Royalist troops. The grounds of Dudley Castle now house the town's zoo. Some of the enclosures' architecture is very retro and is almost as intriguing as the animals on display!

Just next door to the zoo is the Black Country Living Museum, offering an excellent glimpse into the region's past. Trolley Buses, a Victorian Funfair, an ironmonger's forge, a Victorian school and a small coal mine are just some of the experiences to be had. Some of the buildings were dismantled elsewhere and reconstructed on site for the enjoyment and education of visitors. The Museum has been used for filming, most notably for the 'Peaky Blinders' television series.

Next door to the Black Country Museum is the Dudley Canal Trust, showing off some of what locals would call the 'cut'. A small section of Britain's manmade waterways that were carved into the ground during the industrial revolution. Anyone from Dudley would proudly tell you that the town has more miles of canals than Venice. A sign of its prominence as an industrial hub.

If visiting Dudley during winter it is advisable to wrap up warm. If you head east from the Castle you will not find higher ground until you reach the Ural Mountains in Russia.

Venturing a couple of miles south of Dudley to Netherton a large ship's anchor will greet motorists at the side of the road. Manufactured by Hingley, it is a replica of the anchor that was built in the town for the ill-fated RMS Titanic. 100 Yards from the anchor is 'The Old Swan' public house, known informally by locals as 'Ma Pardoes'. This name is in honour of the former Landlady Doris Pardoe. The pub is well worth a visit, not least because of the ale that is brewed on the premises. It is like going back in time to more than a century ago; the décor is gloriously pre-war and the staff are usually dressed in smart shirts or blouses. No 'juke box', no pool table, no modern gimmicks. Just good beer, good food and the company of friendly Black Country folk.

Looking east from the M5 you will see the outskirts of Birmingham – another industrial region. Many people from outside the West Midlands will incorrectly associate the Black Country's towns as being in Birmingham. Indeed they can also make the mistake of assuming the Black Country accent is a Birmingham ('Brummie') one but they are distinct to the locals and there is a rivalry between the two communities that features in all elements of their society: dialect, sport, culture and industry.

One of the 'frontier' communities of the Black Country is Smethwick bordering the City limits. As the M5 meanders westwards it crosses Spon Lane which was the original base of the Chance Brothers' factory. Established in 1824, the factory produced lenses for lighthouses across the world. As well as the all-important lenses, the brothers would in some cases, be responsible for the construction of the lighthouses too. Somewhat ironic given that Smethwick is 70 miles from the sea, but a testament to the availability of skilled workers in the Black Country. The company has since moved to Malvern and now contributes to the field of science offering precision glass for industrial, laboratory and research purposes. The division of the company that preserves lighthouses is now based in Victoria, Australia.

Bewdley

Junction 3: A456 & Birmingham

The M5 crosses the A456, a regional trunk road that connects Birmingham with the A49 at Wooferton at the southern tip of Shropshire. Heading west on the A456 will take motorists near to Stourbridge. As the name suggests, the town grew around a crossing point of the River Stour, a tributary of the River Severn. Stourbridge's traditional industry was glass making and there is a museum dedicated to it at Wollaston. Tudor Crystal is the only remaining glass factory in Stourbridge.

Continuing west is the town of Kidderminster, the capital of the Carpet Industry. Sadly, cheaper foreign competition has diminished Kidderminster's manufacturing prowess to a fraction of what it once was but there are still a small number of firms that produce quality carpets that are sold to luxurious hotels and palaces throughout the world. A museum dedicated to the industry can be found just off the town's ring road.

Another 10 minutes along the A456 and motorists are welcomed to the beautiful town of Bewdley. It used to be the furthest upstream port on the River Severn – Britain's longest river. From Bewdley (and Kidderminster) a

9

heritage steam train can be travelled on along the Severn Valley to Bridgnorth. The line is no longer part of the national rail network following the closures of lines after the 'Beaching Report' in the 1960s.

The Severn Valley Railway at Arley

The 'West Midlands Safari and Leisure Park' is nestled between Kidderminster and Bewdley on the A456. It is home to over 160 species of exotic animals, some of which are endangered. It opened in 1973 and was originally a refuge for retired circus animals. It has grown over the decades to include several specialist enclosures for anything from meerkats to sealions. The safari park is in the grounds of the former stately home, Spring Grove House, which is now a luxury venue for hire.

Heading east from Junction 3, the A456 will take you into the heart of Birmingham within about 20 minutes in light traffic. Barely anything in the city centre is more than 70 years old, the city having been heavily bombed by the Luftwaffe during the Second World War. Like many other cities, post-war architecture was not kind on Birmingham. Even structures built as late as the 1970s are now being torn down and replaced. A prime example was the former Birmingham Central Library, an example of Brutalist Architecture designed by local Architect John Madin, being a predominantly concrete structure which Prince Charles was quoted as saying 'resembles a place where books are incinerated, not kept'. A further massive rebuilding programme has constantly been taking place in the city centre since the war. The second Bull Ring Shopping Centre to be built since 1950s is the centrepiece to a restructuring for the 21st Century. The modernisation programme is so constant that there has never been a street-atlas of Birmingham that has been accurate more than a few weeks.

Birmingham, old and new

A short drive from Junction 3 are the Frankley and Bartley Reservoirs. Both partly supplied with water from the Elan Valley in Mid-Wales. Built by the former 'Birmingham Corporation Water Department', the Elan Aqueduct was the primary source of fresh water for the city since the early 1900s. Purely using the force of gravity, water cascades from the Welsh mountains at 3mph towards the city, crossing the River Severn near Bewdley. As the city has grown the demand on water has grown. As such the Water Board (now Severn Trent) have been working on the Birmingham Resilience Project – a secondary pipeline of water pumped directly from the river near Stourport-on-Severn and then syphoned through a newly-laid pipeline to Frankley.

As the M5 flows south of Junction 3 it quickly leaves behind the conurbation of the Black Country and Birmingham in favour of the green scenery of Worcestershire.

Junctions 4 and 4A: North Worcestershire's Crossroads

The M5 briefly touches the A38, a national trunk road that extends from Bodmin in Cornwall to Mansfield in Nottinghamshire. At 292 miles in length it is the longest 'two digit' A-class road in England. Taking in destinations including Birmingham, Worcester, Bristol, Exeter and Plymouth, it was a precursor for the M5. Indeed, long-experienced drivers will advise that the A38 was always synonymous with congestion and delays and they would usually use older roads to avoid it. In modern times they use the A38 to avoid delays on the M5.

Taking the A38 north from Junction 4 will take motorists into Birmingham along the 'Bristol Road'. Just a couple of miles from the M5 is Longbridge, one of the outer areas of Birmingham. It is now unrecognisable compared to its appearance until the late 1990s when it was dominated by the MG Rover works. Motor vehicles were built on this site from 1906 but by the 2010s it was predominantly a shopping centre. MG Rover had a chequered trading history, undergoing numerous occasions of rebranding and restructuring. Despite various foreign investors trying to resuscitate it during the 1990s and early 2000s, the company that has previously been known as British Leyland, Morris, Austin, Rover and MG finally collapsed by 2010 after its European sales reduced by 96% inside five years.

Aside Junction 4 is a depot belonging to the Highways Agency contractors Ringway. In winter, this is one of the locations from where a fleet of grit lorries takes to the roads to keep them usable for other motorists. This coincidentally means that the roundabout at Junction 4 is one of the most gritted locations in the country!

In under a mile is Junction 4A, the interchange for the M42 that initially heads due east. This can be a particularly busy stretch as it is often used by Worcestershire and Black Country residents commuting to the southern and eastern sides of Birmingham. For those travelling further afield it leads within 9 miles to the M40 – a direct highway to Oxford and London. If motorists continue on the M42 it leads to Birmingham Airport and the National Exhibition Centre and then, eventually, due north-east in the direction of Nottingham.

To the east the Lickey Hills can appear lush on a clear day. The Lickeys contain the steepest railway gradient in Britain between the stations of Bromsgrove and Barnt Green. At 2.65% (1 in 37) the Lickey incline was an obstacle for early generations of steam locomotives. At Bromsgrove railway station locomotives known as 'bankers' were kept to push trains up the incline. One locomotive was built specifically for this in 1919 and was named the Lickey Banker but those who worked with her nicknamed her 'Big Bertha'.

As the M5 flows past the M42 interchange, motorists will see the masts of the Droitwich Transmitting Station at Wychbold. At night-time they are illuminated with red navigation lights to warn low-flying aircraft. The station has been transmitting Long Wave and Medium Wave radio since the 1930s. The Long Wave broadcasting of Radio 4 can be picked up by radios in much of Western Europe this side of the Alps.

Chateau Impney

Junction 5: Droitwich

The A38 passes under the M5 at Junction 5 and bypasses Droitwich towards Worcester. As the suffix 'wich' suggests, the town is famous for the massive concentrations of salt having been extracted there for at least two millennia. The brine water in Droitwich contains 2½ pounds of salt per gallon (0.25 kilograms per litre). This ratio is ten times higher than sea water and is only surpassed by the Dead Sea.

Due to the salt deposits, Droitwich has been an important settlement since the Roman Occupation of Britain. One of the roads leading to the east of the town is called 'Salt Way' and judging by how straight it is it must have Roman origins. A 'salt tax' was levied on the town by successive Monarchs until 1825 as up to 8 tonnes of salt would be extracted from the brine each year. Salt was and is still a valuable commodity and has been known to be used as currency in the past, hence the word 'salary'. A statue of the Salt Workers can be seen next to Droitwich Library.

John Corbett, one of the 'salt barons' of the town used his fortune to build a Louis XIII style chateau complete with landscaped gardens on the edge of the town. It was named Impney Hall. The 106-bedroom stately home had a number of different owners after Corbett's death and it was eventually refurbished as a luxury hotel and venue after the Second World War and renamed 'Chateau Impney'. It is aside the A38 between Junction 5 and Droitwich town centre and was well worth the diversion for afternoon tea for those with money to burn but unfortunately it closed permanently during the Coronavirus Pandemic of 2020.

During the Victorian era, Droitwich established itself as a spa town. The advent of rail travel led to masses of people attending the brine baths, particularly for their wonderful medical benefits in terms of muscular relief and soothing. They also contained the warmest natural water in Britain outside another Roman settlement: Bath. Unfortunately, the brine baths in the town have been closed since 2008.

Other water-based features of the town are the Lido and the Canal. The Lido originally used diluted brine water as the salt would negate the need for further cleansing chemicals such as Chlorine. When first opened in the 1930s, the pool was heated to the same temperature as the Mediterranean Sea and the Lido was marketed as 'the seaside has come to Droitwich Spa'. The Droitwich Barge Canal was built by James Brindley and connected the town with the River Severn near Claines. It was an essential route for the transport of salt before the railways.

Motorists that use the A38 to drive towards Bromsgrove from Junction 5 will pass the Avoncroft Museum. This attraction claims to be the oldest open-air museum in Britain. It has 30 examples of historic buildings on display, some of them date back to medieval times. Many of them were deconstructed elsewhere and rebuilt in the museum, the rest are reconstructions based on historic design documents. The Avoncroft Museum also looks after historic buildings elsewhere in Worcestershire as the organisation is keen to keep them in their original location. Where this is not possible, the building will be carefully moved to the museum estate.

Junction 6: Six Ways

Six Ways is the home of Worcester Warriors Rugby Football Club. A modern enclosed stadium that is worthy of Worcester's history and prestige. The name 'Six Ways' comes from the motorway junction: the A449 link road, the A4440 to Warndon, the two directions of 'Pershore Lane' (south to Pershore, north to Droitwich) and the north and south carriageways of the M5.

A mile or so behind the stadium is Hindlip Hall. The original Hindlip Hall dated back to the late 16th Century and was the scene of plotting in both the Babington Plot against Elizabeth I and the Gunpowder Plot against James I. It is with some irony that the site is now dedicated to 'law and order' and is now the Headquarters of West Mercia Police. The current Hall was built in 1820 and like many stately homes had various owners and functions until its current use. In 1940 it was taken over by the Ministry of Works and designated as a potential base of operations for the War Cabinet. It has been owned by public organisations ever since.

A stone's throw from Six Ways is a factory belonging to Worcester-Bosch. Formerly Worcester Engineering, the factory produces heating systems, boilers and solar panels. It was acquired by the German Bosch group in the 1990s but retained its identity, hence the hyphenated name.

The tomb of King John at Worcester Cathedral

Junction 7: Worcester

Heading east from Junction 7, motorists will head towards the towns of Pershore and Evesham, both on the banks of one of the Avons – the M5 crosses two. Pershore is noted for its Plum Festival and has an abbey that was re-consecrated as a parish during the reign of Henry VIII. Historians will know that the King wanted to divorce his first wife, Catherine of Aragon, but this was not permitted by Pope Clement VII. In order to progress his divorce, Henry VIII declared his autonomy over religious matters, setting up the Church of England in what has become known as the Reformation. All Roman Catholic assets throughout England were seized and suffered one of three fates: re-consecration as Anglican Parish Churches, deconstruction, or they were sold off. There are numerous examples of consequences of the Reformation all along the M5. Evesham is another example of such a place, the abbey was deconstructed, leaving only the bell tower standing.

West of Junction 7 is the grand city of Worcester. One of the smaller cities in Britain it is easily explored in a day and for those who enjoy shopping is well worth a visit. It has a terrific balance of small independent traders along with larger chain stores.

Worcester is home to the oldest newspaper in continuous production in the English-speaking world. Founded in 1690 as the 'Worcester Post-Man' by Stephen Bryan. In 1740, the newspaper was bought by the Berrow family. By 1753 it was renamed the 'Berrow's Worcester Journal', and is known as this to this day. It is currently owned by the Newsquest Media Group.

The Cathedral is the resting place for three key figures from our history. In 1216 King John was interred there a year after signing the Magna Carta at Runneymede. Widely considered to be one of the early steps towards democracy in England, the Magna Carta curbed some of the King's taxation and made provision for a 'fair trial'.

Ten feet from King John's tomb is that of Prince Arthur, the eldest son of Henry VII. He died before his father and so never ascended to the throne. Incidentally Arthur was the first husband of Catherine of Aragon and the ceremony took place by proxy further up the Severn at Bewdley. Prince Henry (later Henry VIII) had to seek permission from the Pope to marry his brother's widow so it was with some irony that he eventually asked the Pope for permission to divorce her. Historians can only hypothesise how Britain's history would have differed if Arthur had been King and not Henry VIII.

The Bewdley connection with the Cathedral continues into more recent history as it is also where the ashes of Stanley Baldwin are interred along with those of his wife Lucy. Stanley Baldwin was born in a house of Lower Park in Bewdley and served as the town's Member of Parliament between

1908 and 1937. He led the Conservative Party between 1923 and 1937 and was Prime Minister during three non-consecutive terms. Three things he tends to be remembered for are his supposed failure to prepare Britain against the rise of continental fascism, his Government's increasing the supply of electricity to domestic properties four-fold and the abdication of Edward VIII. Like all political figures, he divides opinion.

In centuries past, many people in Worcester were employed for the manufacturing of gloves. Certain select glove-makers have operated in the city until recently. The gloves worn by Elizabeth II at her coronation in 1953 were made in Worcester. St Andrews Church on the Deansway is named 'the Glover's Needle' by locals due to its narrow spire that rises 245 feet.

On the other side of the River Severn from The Glover's Needle and The Cathedral, cricket fans can find one of the most scenic grounds in the country. New Road, the home of Worcestershire County Cricket Club has a wonderful backdrop being aside the mighty Severn and opposite the Cathedral. The former can be a nuisance though as in times of flood the pitch is submerged.

The Malverns

Beyond Junction 7: The Malverns and Bredon Hill.

Immediately after Junction 7, motorists get a panoramic view of the Malvern Hills. They form part of the boundary between Worcestershire and Herefordshire, with a small section in Gloucestershire at the southern end. There are 22 peaks of the hills in all, the highest being the Worcestershire Beacon at 1,394 feet above sea level. On a clear day, views of up to 40 miles can be enjoyed in all directions. There are numerous towns and villages that make up the community in and around the Malverns. Great Malvern is one of the few places in the country that still has gas-powered street lighting. Malvern Link is the home of the hand-built sports car: Morgan, and Little Malvern is the resting place for the composer: Sir Edward Elgar. Most of the length of the Malverns can be enjoyed by simply following the A449 south of Worcester.

Sir Edward Elgar was a local man, born in 1857 at Lower Broadheath just west of Worcester and lived with his wife, Alice, in Great Malvern until his death in 1934. His music is widely recognised to this day as it is usually played at events of national significance as well as being in the collection of any lover of classical music. As well as music, Elgar was a lover of football and a keen cyclist. He used to cycle from Malvern to Wolverhampton on a regular basis to watch Wolves play football at Molineux.

Six miles after Junction 7, Bredon Hill comes into view to the east. On the west side of Bredon Hill, outside the village of Bredon's Norton is Norton Park, another stately home that belonged to Victoria Woodhull Martin between 1901 and her death in 1927. Victoria Woodhull was an American citizen who led quite a colourful career, being as she was the first female Stockbroker on Wall Street and the first female candidate for President of the United States in the 1872 election. Woodhull moved to Britain in 1877 after divorcing her second husband. In 1883 she married John Martin of the banking dynasty. After his death in 1901, Victoria Woodhull Martin, as she was then known, retired to Bredon Hill where she volunteered herself as a teacher in the village school at Bredon's Norton. There is a memorial plaque honouring her in Tewkesbury Abbey.

A few hundred yards before Junction 8 is Strensham Services, which opened in 1962. The location is notable because the first section of the M5 to be built and only initially only connected Birmingham and the M50. This will be explained in the section on Junction 8. The north-bound services are of note because their nearest neighbour is a base for the Midlands Air Ambulance – one of three in the region covered by the West Midlands Ambulance Service.

Junction 8: The Highway into Wales

The interchange for the M50 was a vital transport hub for Britain in the early 1960s. Until the opening of the first Severn Crossing in 1966, the M50 was the most direct motorway into South Wales from London, the south and the Midlands. Before then, major trunk roads such as the A40, A48, A46 and A49 as well as connecting roads like the A449 and A456 were the choice of routes for motorists from such locations. All these routes had bottlenecks as they ran through the centre of cities and towns like Gloucester, Worcester, Bewdley, Malvern etc. Vehicles such as coaches, buses and lorries were gradually increasing in size and weight. In addition to this, research by the RAC suggests that in 1951 less than 10% of households in Britain owned a car. By 1971 that had increased to 44%. Britain clearly needed four times as many roads!

The M50 was one of the first motorways to open in 1960, although the section between Junction 1 and the M5 was not completed until the first section of the M5 opened in 1962. Relieving the ever-increasing congestion on places like Gloucester and Worcester (and many other locations up and down the country) was a priority for governments of the day. The M5 and M50 were essential to that strategy.

Whilst Britain's car industry and sale market were growing at unprecedented rates during the 1960s, and the motorway network was also taking shape, this would spell disaster for many businesses. For instance, before the motorways were built one possible route to South Wales from the Black Country and Birmingham would be the A456 and A49. Coach drivers and passengers, lorry drivers and other motorists were the lifeblood of many cafes at the side of these roads as well as in the towns they connected. The prospect of driving at speeds of up to 70mph for hours on end meant such cafes saw their customers disappear overnight. Most long-experienced motorists would agree that modern Motorway Service Areas in Britain have never been able to provide the same quality and variety of food that motorists could find in roadside cafés.

Flooded Tewkesbury

Junction 9: Tewkesbury & Ashchurch

A couple of miles before the Junction, the M5 crosses the first of its two Avons. This is arguably the more famous as it flows through Stratford-upon-Avon, a town that attracts 3 million visitors per year due to it being the birthplace of William Shakespeare.

After periods of significant rainfall, the Avon can appear to be half a mile wide in the vicinity of the M5. The area is particularly vulnerable to flooding due to its confluence with the Severn near Tewkesbury at which point it is tidal. The Severn flows into the Bristol Channel, which has the second highest tide in the world – 49 feet between its highest and lowest points. This means that at times of high tide, it pushes water upstream as far as Upton-on-Severn in Worcestershire. Upton is particularly prone to flooding for the same reason as the stretch of the Avon that flows under the M5 simply because when the tide is high there is nowhere for rainwater from upstream to escape to. The tidal impact of the Bristol Channel is evident at various points near to the M5.

Tewkesbury is just a mile from Junction 9. In times of flood it can be completely cut off from the M5 – unless motorists take a detour along the A38 from Worcester. It is a very pleasant place to visit with quite a substantial retail centre for a town of its size. It is a delight for shoppers, the variety of stores has something for everyone and it is rather unique in that it has had no 'redevelopment' like many other shopping districts. It is quite likely that Tewkesbury's appearance is the same in the 2020s as it was in the 1820s. Many of the buildings having timber frames, preserved from the Middle Ages.

ERECTED TO THE MEMORY OF
VICTORIA WOODHULL MARTIN
AN AMERICAN CITIZEN
LONG RESIDENT IN THIS NEIGHBOURHOOD
WHO DEVOTED HERSELF UNSPARINGLY TO ALL
THAT COULD PROMOTE THE GREAT CAUSE OF
ANGLO-AMERICAN FRIENDSHIP
BORN 23 SEPTEMBER 1838 DIED 9 JUNE 1927

Tewkesbury Abbey

Tewkesbury Abbey is just a short walk from the retail area of the town. Founded in 1121, it was one of the Roman Catholic assets that survived the Reformation in the 1530s and was re-consecrated as an Anglican Parish Church. The memorial plaque dedicated to Victoria Woodhull Martin is located under the south-east window. (See section about Beyond Junction 7)

Tewkesbury was also the site of one of the decisive battles of the Wars of the Roses. In 1471 it was the place of victory for the House of York resulting in Edward IV being restored to the throne, after defeating Henry VI, who had displaced him just six months earlier. Henry VI and Edward IV are the only two English monarchs to have served for two reigns, Henry VI 1422-1461 and 1470-1471 and Edward VI 1461-1470 and 1471-1482.

Just east of Junction 9 is the village of Ashchurch, a predominantly an industrial area. There are a few manufacturers in Ashchurch that provide components for the aviation industry. The county of Gloucestershire is widely considered as the 'Cradle of Aviation'. The largest premises in Aschurch is 'Ashchurch Camp', the primary vehicle storage facility for the Ministry of Defence, being home to anything from soft-skin cars to heavy armoured tanks. Some of the buildings on the 178-acre site have internal humidity controls to keep the vehicles in optimum condition.

Junction 10: Cheltenham Spa

A settlement dating back to the Roman occupation of Britain, Cheltenham was established as a stopover between London and South Wales for travellers that had just journeyed over the Cotswolds – or that were just about to. Its location meant it was an important transport hub before the advent of the motorways. Before becoming part of what is now National Express, Black & White Coaches used Cheltenham as a major interchange for long distance coach services.

During the 18th Century a mineral spring was discovered in Cheltenham, establishing it as a Spa Town. Such inland resorts became reasonably popular during the Napoleonic Wars with wealthy people who were unable to holiday on the continent due to the French fleet blockading Britain. As such the investment during the late 18th and early 19th Centuries is evident to this day with Regency-style architecture charming the oldest part of town, particularly in Montpellier area. In Imperial Gardens, tourists can admire a statue of the composer Gustav Holst who was born in the town.

Cheltenham also further underlines Gloucestershire's claim to be the 'Cradle of Aviation' as it is where the first British jet aircraft, the Gloster E.28/39 prototype was built in 1941. Its success led to the first generation of jet aircraft entering service with the Royal Air Force in 1944: the Gloster Meteor. Thousands of Meteors were built and sold to allied air forces. Many were operated for several decades. The headquarters of Gloster were at the village of Hucclecote, not far from Junction 11A.

A further connection with the Defence of the Realm is Government Communications Headquarters (GCHQ), its main facilities being in Cheltenham. It is a Security Service that monitors all varieties communications traffic and then supplies intelligence to the British Armed Forces and associated Security Services. Radio signals, text messages, emails, telephone calls and even postal services are monitored by GCHQ as part of the Ministry of Defence's aim to keep the country safe from enemies, foreign and domestic. GCHQ has specialists on site that can translate communications in over 30 languages. This function is available 24 hours each day, 7 days per week, all year round. It is also responsible for defending the British government against cyber-attacks and some aspects of electronic warfare.

Formerly the Government Code & Cypher School (GC&CS) until 1946, the headquarters were primarily in London until the move to Cheltenham in 1951. Arguably the most famous insight into the work of GCHQ is what is now known about the work of Station X at Bletchley Park in Buckinghamshire that was responsible for deciphering communications of the axis powers during the Second World War. This involved the building of a machine designed by Alan Turing that could decipher the coded transmissions of the German ENIGMA machines. The machine 'Bombe' was widely considered to be the world's first computer as it used the first 'algorithms'. Consequently, Turing is now considered to be the Father of computer science. He was appointed an Officer of the Order of the British Empire in 1946, although the reasons were not made public at the time. His accomplishments were never recognised during his lifetime as his work was hidden by the Official Secrets Act until the early 1990s.

To the north of the town is Cheltenham Racecourse where the annual Gold Cup is contested. Part of the 'Cheltenham Festival', the race usually takes place close to St Patrick's Day because it is particularly popular with Irish visitors. The Cheltenham Gold Cup was controversial in 2020 as it took place during the Coronavirus Pandemic. Britain was not in lockdown until a week after, however the government had advised against large gatherings of people and non-essential travel. Newspaper articles reported that hundreds of people who had attended the event later complained of symptoms of the virus and the organisers were criticised for providing a large opportunity for the virus to spread.

Gloucester Cathedral

Junction 11: Gloucester & the Royal Forest of Dean

The third Cathedral City heading south along the M5, Gloucester has plenty of history. It being the lowest crossing on the River Severn until 1966 has made it a city of strategic importance for the multiple civilizations that have controlled England over the millennia. Until the opening of the M50 in 1962, Gloucester was unavoidable for traffic heading to South Wales from London, and the southern counties. Although on a slightly different route today, the A40 trunk road still wraps around the northern side of Gloucester, Fishguard and London being the west and east terminuses respectively. The A40 is the tallest of the three fly-overs at Junction 11, connecting Cheltenham and Gloucester.

The Cathedral is the epicentre of Gloucester's rich history that has been steered by five monarchs. Henry II granted Gloucester its charter in 1155, granting its citizens equal rights to those of London and Winchester. A ten-year-old Henry III was crowned in the Chapter House of the Cathedral in 1216 after the death of King John who was interred at Worcester Cathedral. The deposed Edward II was entombed in the Cathedral in 1327. Edward II had the distinction of being the first heir to the English Throne to hold the title Prince of Wales after he was born at Caernarfon Castle. Richard II convened sessions of Parliament at Gloucester Cathedral from 1378 and these continued into the reign of Henry IV until 1406.

A stained glass window within the Cathedral dates to the 13th Century and depicts what appears to be a game of golf. This is rather a curious feature as the window predates any other record of the game having been played by three centuries. Another aspect of the Cathedral's architecture is that it attracts crews for film and television. Several of the Harry Potter films had scenes filmed in the Crypt as well as an episode of Sherlock. In the 1990s a short BBC television series called The Choir was filmed in and around the city, charting the rise to fame of a fictitious boy that sang in the Cathedral choir.

A few minutes' walk from the Cathedral is Gloucester Docks, a former bustling inland port. The high tide of the Bristol Channel made sailing in and out of Gloucester a treacherous journey and so the docks were connected by the Gloucester and Sharpness ship canal in 1827. Now primarily a museum piece, fifteen Victorian era warehouses overlook the former quayside. A large portion of it has been redeveloped in recent years as a modern enclosed shopping centre, complete with restaurant chains and a cinema. Sadly, the shopping centre is disconnected from the traditional retail area of the city centre and the impact of this can been seen in the older parts of the centre.

To the north of the City Centre is the Kingsholm Stadium, home of Gloucester Rugby Club. The stadium opened in 1891 but has been modernised in recent years. It has hosted international matches, most recently in the 2015 World Cup. Gloucester are currently in the Premiership and have played in the top tier of English Rugby since the formation of a professional league in 1987.

Famous individuals from Gloucester include Robert Raikes who was one of the founding fathers of the Sunday School movement. The Winter Olympic ski jumper Michael Edwards, better known as 'Eddie the Eagle' was born in Cheltenham and used to practise his skiing at the dry slope to the south of the city which is visible from the M5 after Junction 11A. Two infamous individuals who resided in the city were Fred and Rose West who were both arrested in 1994 and charged with murder. Fred West hung himself whilst on remand, but Rose stood trial in 1995 and was convicted for ten murders. It is suspected that they were responsible for more.

Twice a day, the Severn Bore can be viewed from bridges on the west side of the city. This is a wonderful phenomenon that occurs due to the high tide of the Bristol Channel coupled with the sudden narrowing of the Severn Estuary in a relatively short stretch. The 'maximum bore' occurs on the three days after a full moon when the height of the tide is affected most by the lunar cycle. The bore can be up to 10 feet high on these days, but this depends on several other geographical factors, not least the weather.

West of Gloucester and across the Severn is the Royal Forest of Dean. This elevated rural area is visible between junctions 10 and 14 on a clear day. It has had a Royal suffix since 1066 when it was designated a Royal hunting ground by the Normans. Livestock in the forest were hunted over the centuries either by members of the Royal family or their servants procuring fresh meat for the dinner tables in Royal Households.

Eventually the Royal Forest of Dean became an important mining area due to its rich deposits of coal and iron ore. Edward I passed a series of laws in the early 1300s that protected the rights of 'freeminers' who would supply his army with the raw materials to produce weapons. This was of significance in the Royal Forest of Dean where the most prominent occupation was the mining of coal and iron ore. Freeminers were important in the Middle Ages as they would mine the land they lived on as opposed to working in large industrial pits that would become common during the Industrial Revolution. The rights of freeminers were so highly regarded that when all coal mines were nationalised in 1946, freeminers in the Royal Forest of Dean were excluded.

Royal interest in the forest peaked in 1676 when The Speech House was built. This had two functions, firstly as a hunting lodge for Charles II and secondly as a house of representatives for local freeminers – hence the name. The Speech House survives to this date and is now leased as a hotel. The landlord is the Crown Estate. The wider forest is still largely in public ownership and is maintained by the Forestry Commission.

A further natural resource from the Royal Forest of Dean is timber. It was said that it was the finest timber for shipbuilding. Indeed, Lord Admiral Nelson used to make regular visits to the area to survey the supply of timber to the Royal Navy. His early visits to the area were accompanied by Lord and Lady Hamilton and his later visits were accompanied by just Lady Hamilton. There are many records and personal effects that belonged to Nelson on display in a museum in Monmouth.

Gloster Javelin at RAF Cosford

Junction 11A: From Chariots to Aircraft

This junction was added in the mid-1990s to connect the M5 with the A417, relieving congestion in Gloucester and Tewkesbury. The A417 follows the route of the former Roman Road, Ermine Way, connecting Gloucester with Cirencester and the Fosse Way. Ermine Way is still in use and runs 800 yards parallel and south of the A417 when the M5 crosses them both.

Further underlining the reason why Gloucestershire is the 'Cradle of Aviation', Ermine Way passes through the villages of Hucclecote and Brockworth. The former containing the headquarters and the latter containing the primary airfield for the Gloster Aircraft Company. Of course, the name of the company was pronounced the same as the city, but it was spelled differently because it was considered the name 'Gloucester' would cause mispronunciation and confusion amongst foreign customers. Gloster was absorbed by the Hawker Siddeley Corporation in 1963, which in turn was nationalised as British Aerospace in 1977.

The eastbound A417 takes motorists very quickly into the Cotswolds, ascending over 900 feet in three miles to the famous Air Balloon roundabout at Birdlip. The Air Balloon is a public house just outside the village and is a popular stopping place for walkers. It was opened in 1784 and was probably named after one of the first British hydrogen balloon flights that took place that year between Berkeley and Kingscote. A further reason that Gloucestershire is the 'Cradle of Aviation'. Within a few minutes' walk of the pub, there are breathtakingly beautiful views across the county of Gloucestershire, towards the Royal Forest of Dean.

Continuing along the A417 for around 15 minutes will lead to Cirencester. An important Roman settlement and at one time was the largest outside London. The Fosse Way and Ermine Way pass through the town making it of vital strategic value. The Fosse Way was one of the major arterial roads built by the Romans, connecting Exeter with Lincoln. 230 miles in length, it is a fine example of a direct route. If a straight line were drawn on a map of Britain between Exeter and Lincoln, the Fosse Way would not stray more than six miles from that line. The M5 crosses the Fosse Way at Junction 29.

Modern Cirencester is a worthwhile diversion with good venues for food and drink, a surprisingly large retail area and a museum about Corinium – the Roman name for the town. The centre is dominated by the tall tower of the Church of St John the Baptist, informally known as the 'Cathedral of the Cotswolds'. To the west of the town is the Royal Agricultural University, the Patron of which is usually the British monarch, although, this role has been held by the Prince of Wales since 1982. He also has a private residence a few miles away at Highgrove.

The A417 dual carriageway south of Cirencester is reclassed as the A419. This road is a common route from the M5 area to the counties along the mid-south coast, particularly Dorset, Hampshire and Sussex. The next sizeable town beyond Cirencester is Cricklade, dating to the Saxon era of Britain. It is very close to the source of the Thames, the longest river wholly within in England.

One mile to the west of Junction 11A is a factory that produces ice cream on behalf of Walls. Ice Cream is one of two famous foodstuffs that is associated with the City, the other being cheese. Both Single and Double Gloucester cheese should be produced using milk from cows bred within the county and the colour is supposed to be like that of Cotswold Stone.

The local production of cheese is celebrated every Spring Bank Holiday with a 'cheese rolling' event taking place on Coopers Hill. This is a dangerous event where participants roll a 7-9lb round of cheese 200 yards down the hill with a gradient of 50% and then chase after it. The cheese can reach speeds of up to 70 mph which can be lethal if it collides with spectators. Coopers Hill is to the east of the M5 about a mile after Junction 11A.

A couple of miles beyond Coopers Hill is the town of Painswick. The Parish Church of St Mary's is famous for the attractive yew trees in its Rococo Gardens. Legend has it that no more than 99 trees can survive because whenever a 100th tree is planted, another one perishes.

Javelin Park

Junction 12: Javelin Park

This junction primarily serves traffic heading into Gloucester from the south. The feature that is unmissable at Junction 12 is Javelin Park Energy from Waste facility. It has been operational since autumn 2019 and burns 190,000 tonnes of household waste per year in an 'environmentally friendly' process on behalf of the local authority. The residual steam drives turbines that generate electricity for the national grid.

The name of the facility is derived from the last aircraft to bear the Gloster name prior to its amalgamation with Hawker Siddeley. The Gloster Javelin was an interceptor that was flown by the RAF from 1956 to 1968. It was withdrawn from service as the nation's primary interceptor and replaced by the English Electric Lightening, a supersonic jet and twice as fast as the Javelin.

Gloster Javelins used to take off from the former base, RAF Moreton Vallance, the site where the Energy from Waste facility is now built. Continuing 500 yards along the M5 motorists can see sections of the old runway aside the carriageway.

Tetbury

Junction 13: Stroud, the Severn Estuary & the Southern Cotswolds

There are several places of interest within a short drive of Junction 13. On the west side of the M5 are the communities of Slimbridge and Berkeley. Slimbridge has a designated nature reserve aside the River Severn, designed to protect bird habitats, specifically wild fowl. The reserve was the first of nine to be established in Britain by the Wildfowl & Wetlands Trust (WWT), an organisation founded by Sir Peter Scott. Sir Peter was the son of Robert Falcon Scott, better known as Scott of the Antarctic.

Inspired by his father, Sir Peter Scott took a keen interest in natural history and set up the WWT at Slimbridge in 1946 as a centre where the public could observe the more scientific aspects of conservation. His influence on natural science did not end there as he became involved in the founding of the World Wildlife Fund and is even credited with drawing the panda in the logo.

Five miles down the A38 from Slimbridge is Berkeley, a small town dominated by its castle and the now decommissioned nuclear power station. The castle was built in the 12th Century and has been owned by the Berkeley family since it was founded. Initially built to defend against incursions across the Severn Estuary into England by the Welsh, the castle soon settled into a role as the Berkeley family's stately home. In the early 14th Century the castle was briefly occupied by Edward II after he had been deposed by his inner circle of advisors. It was a brief stay as he was murdered with a white-hot poker.

Edward II had been overthrown following his disastrous and humiliating defeat at the Battle of Bannockburn near Stirling. The English armies outnumbered the Scots by more than 3:1 but were decisively beaten by the natives led by Robert the Bruce in 1314. This ensured Scotland and England remained separate Kingdoms until James VI of Scotland succeeded Elizabeth I in 1603.

The scientist, Edward Jenner, was born in Berkeley. He is the 'father of immunisation' as he pioneered the vaccination process against Smallpox. He experimented with transferring the pus from cowpox blisters to a healthy individual and then later placed them into close quarters with someone suffering with smallpox. The experiment was a success and so cowpox bacteria were eventually used to vaccinate large sections of the community. Until Jenner's vaccine, Smallpox killed around a tenth of the British population. Within a few years it was eradicated in Britain and in 1979 the World Health Organisation declared Smallpox had been eradicated from the world.

Jenner's scientific exploits were not confined to medicine. He was also interested in aviation and was one of the early pioneers of balloon flight. In 1784 he successfully flew beneath a hydrogen balloon from Berkeley Castle to Kingscote Park, owned by Anthony Kingscote, who later became Jenner's father-in-law. Jenner's scientific achievements brought him to the attention of King George IV who appointed him as his 'extraordinary physician'.

Berkeley was chosen as the location for Britain's first commercially owned nuclear power station due to it being aside the Severn Estuary, an uninterrupted supply of natural water being an essential element in the cooling process. Construction began in 1956 and the two reactors began generating electricity in 1962 and continued until they went offline in 1989. All of the remaining fuel had been removed by 1992 however the equipment and the reactors are currently encased in concrete that cannot be demolished until the late 2070s owing to the risk of radiation.

To the east of Junction 13 is Stroud, one of the more industrial towns in the Cotswold area. This does not detract from the pleasantness of the town. Like all towns in and around the Cotswolds, Stroud's destiny was influenced heavily by the wool trade, in this instance the manufacturing of wool/cloth items. In the late 18th Century the town used to produce the familiar scarlet tunics for the British Army. In later centuries the town mills produced the green cloth that covered Billiard tables, an industry that experienced a revival in the 1970s when Britain's households started watching colour television and televised snooker matches were discernible. Tennis balls are also manufactured in the town.

Stroud also has a connection to every British child who developed an interest in railways, as from 1965 it was the home of Rev Wilbert Awdry until his death in 1997. The rail enthusiast and author is best remembered for creating the world of Thomas the Tank Engine and Friends, a series of books set on the fictional island of Sodor. The stories have been adapted to audio books, television series and films and have developed a wide variety of merchandise over the decades.

A little further south of Stroud is Dursley, a pleasant market town at the foot of the Cotswolds. The name of the town is very familiar to fans of the Harry Potter books and films as it was used as the name of the eponymous hero's adopted family. The author, J.K. Rowling was born in Yate, a village a few miles further south of Dursley.

On the A38 between Dursley and Stroud is the village of Cambridge, not to be confused with the University city, this one is pronounced as if there are two 'm's. It is so named because the River Cam flows through it on its way to converging with the Severn.

Motorists who drive along the A4135 beyond Dursley, towards Tetbury, ascend very quickly into the Cotswolds. At the top of the hill, excellent views across the Severn Estuary can be seen on a clear day. Tetbury is also a pleasant market town with a traditional Market House at its centre. Local attractions include a Police museum and two nearby stately homes: Highgrove and Chavenage. As mentioned in the section on Junction 11A, Highgrove is a private residence belonging to the Duchy of Cornwall, Prince

Charles and Camilla being tenants for life. Chavenage is an Elizabethan house owned by the same family since that time. It was used in both World Wars for hosting allied forces and it is credited for being the location from where aircraft of the Royal Australian Air Force first flew. It is an extremely attractive building that has been used numerous times for filming televisions series, including Lark Rise to Candleford, Poldark, Casualty and Poirot.

Following the B4060 south of Dursley takes motorists to Wotton-Under-Edge, past the Tyndale monument. The monument seen clearly to the east of the M5 between Junction 13 and Michaelwood motorway services is a memorial to William Tyndale who was a protestant preacher during the 16th Century from whom Henry VIII took a great deal of influence when founding the Church of England. Despite being a protestant, he became an enemy of the King for opposing the annulment of his marriage to Catherine of Aragon. Tyndale escaped to the continent, hoping to find refuge with the supporters of Martin Luther but he was arrested near Brussels and burned at the stake on a charge of heresy. The charge was a consequence of him translating the bible into English. By 1611, the King James Bible was published and the scholars who contributed to it drew heavily from Tyndale's work.

Junction 14: Oldbury-on-Severn & Charfield

This is probably one of the less busy junctions on the M5 in terms of volume of traffic. In October 2009 it featured in the national headlines due to a gruesome discovery. Highway Maintenance teams were clearing vegetation and litter at the side of one of the slip roads to the junction when they found a bag full of human bones. Testing established that they were the remains of Melanie Hall, a woman who had disappeared after a night out in Bath in 1996. No one has ever been convicted of her murder.

Turning east takes motorists to Charfield, a small village not far from the motorway. The main rail line between Birmingham and Bristol passes through the village although trains have not stopped there since the station closed in the 1960s. Nevertheless, Charfield does feature prominently in the history of British Railways due to a crash that occurred in the village in 1928. Fifteen people were killed in an explosion when a freight train and mail train collided. Amongst the dead were two children who were never identified. They were laid to rest in the Parish Churchyard. Locals claim that, occasionally, a woman dressed in black would arrive at the churchyard in a chauffeur-driven Rolls Royce to lay flowers on the children's grave but her identity, and that of the children, was never established.

To the west of the M5 is Thornbury. Parts of the town have views across the Severn Estuary towards Chepstow and the southern reaches of the Royal Forest of Dean. A couple of miles beyond Thornbury is another former nuclear power station at Oldbury-on-Severn. The first of its two reactors began generating electricity in 1967 and the plant was still generating electricity until 2012 when the decommissioning process began. As with all nuclear power stations, it will be around 80-90 years before radiation levels are sufficiently reduced to allow complete clearance of the site. Demolition of the structures at Oldbury is scheduled to take place in 2101. Due to its futuristic nature, Oldbury was used for filming of two BBC science-fiction series in the 1970s: Doctor Who and Blake's 7.

Severn Bridge

Junction 15: The Almondsbury Interchange & the Severn Crossings.

This is a major interchange between the M5 and the M4. Turning eastbound will take motorists to the M32 within a couple of miles, the most 'direct' route into the centre of Bristol, but it can be very congested at peak times. It is also a useful route into the centre of Bath via the A4174. If travelling to Bristol by bus or coach the M32 can be an advantage though as there is a dedicated bus lane into the city centre.

Traveling further east on the M4 will eventually lead to Swindon, Reading, Windsor and London. Turning west takes motorists across the Severn Estuary into Wales and then the M4 continues to the cities of Newport, Cardiff and Swansea. There are two motorway crossings over the Severn Estuary, the Severn Bridge and the Prince of Wales Bridge.

The Severn Bridge opened in 1966, replacing the M50 as the lowest road crossing over the Severn, saving a detour of two and a half hours. It linked the village of Aust in England with the town of Chepstow in Wales. Prior to the bridge being completed, there was a car ferry that operated between Aust and Beachley on the English side of the Wye. The service was far from reliable because it could only carry up to 17 cars but no goods vehicles or buses. And it was vulnerable to the rise and fall of the tide in the Bristol Channel as well as the prevailing sands within the water.

Once completed, the full extent of the bridge crosses two river estuaries, the second being the Wye. According to BBC News Archives, traffic began to queue up to cross the bridge up to four days prior to Queen Elizabeth II declaring it open on 8th September 1966. Amongst the motorists queuing up were a pair of newlyweds returning from their honeymoon, spending each night sleeping in the car!

Construction cost £8 million (£151 million accounting for inflation) between 1961 and 1966 and this has been recouped by toll charges on the crossing until December 2018. The tolls were initially collected in both directions but controversially they were altered in 1992 to charge vehicles entering Wales whilst vehicles entering England could cross without charge. As mentioned in the section about Junction 8, car ownership in Britain increased fourfold between when the Severn Bridge was initially planned and a few years after its completion. Also, the weight of increasingly large vehicles put strain on the structure and so weight restrictions were placed in the outer lanes. It soon became clear that one bridge was not enough to cope with the traffic on this route and so in the 1980s planning began for a second crossing.

Work on the Second Severn Crossing began in April 1992 and it was opened by the Prince of Wales in June 1996. It was built three miles downstream of the first bridge. Like the original bridge it was also funded by tolls, but these ended in 2018 on both bridges. Its renaming as 'The Prince of Wales Bridge' did not occur until 2018 to coincide with Prince Charles celebrating being Prince of Wales for 60 years – the longest any one has held the title. The M4 was rerouted to cross the new bridge and the first bridge was re-designated as the M48.

The route of the Prince of Wales Bridge is no more than 500 yards from that of the Severn Tunnel. This was built for the Great Western Railway and completed in 1886. At 4.3 miles long the tunnel was the longest in Britain until the opening of the Channel Tunnel in 1994. It was also the longest under water tunnel in the world until 1984. It is still in use today, being the most direct rail route between London and South Wales. Work was undertaken to electrify the tunnel in 2016 so that the most modern trains could use it. Due to its age, around 11 million gallons of water are pumped out of the tunnel each day and it is claimed the tunnel would fill with water in 26 minutes if the pumps and backup systems were switched off.

Concorde at Bristol Aerospace

Junction 16: Filton & Bristol

Immediately after the Almondsbury Interchange is Junction 16. Another junction where the A38 crosses the M5, it is another route into the centre of Bristol but somewhat 'stop-start' compared to the M4/M32 as it crosses many sets of traffic lights. The mouth of the Severn Tunnel can be seen from the A38 a short distance from Junction 16. Firstly, the road passes through Filton, a town in South Gloucestershire, although many are forgiven for thinking that it is a suburb of Bristol.

Filton is another reason that Gloucestershire is the 'cradle of aviation'. BAE Systems, Airbus, Rolls Royce, MBDA and GKN are all major employers in the town, and it is where arguably the most famous civilian aircraft was built: Concorde. Including the prototypes, only twenty of the supersonic airliners were built because the project was a commercial failure. The greatest leaps forward for aviation technology took place in the 1950s and 1960s. This was due to intense competition between the global powers of the time: The United States of America, the Union of Soviet Socialist Republics, the United Kingdom and France. Whilst the first two were also embroiled in the space race, all four were also major players in developing jet engines and breaking the sound barrier. Simultaneous to landing people on the moon, the countries were also in a race to build a commercial airliner that could travel faster than the speed of sound. Concorde first flew on 2nd March 1969, four and half months before Neil Armstrong walked on the moon.

Concorde was a joint venture between the British Aircraft Corporation and Sud-Aviation of France, and it was a huge success, flying at Mach 2 (twice the speed of sound / 1,354mph). The American equivalent never flew commercially whilst the Soviet Tupolev-144 only flew commercially for eight years. Concorde's scientific success was quickly followed by commercial failure. Orders for Concorde were placed by sixteen different airlines throughout the world, but these were cancelled by early 1973 for two main reasons. Firstly, the oil crisis at the time made airlines cautious about running aircraft with a high consumption rate for fuel. Secondly, the authorities at New York's JFK Airport would not permit Concorde to land there, deeming it to be 'too loud'. As New York is one of the most popular destinations in the world for tourists and business travellers alike, the sixteen would-be purchasers of Concorde lost interest and became more interested in aircraft that could fly into New York. Orders were instead placed for the new wide-bodied and more fuel-efficient Boeing 747.

The fourteen commercial Concordes that were built were never sold. Seven were loaned to Air France and seven to British Airways who both began operating them in 1976. Recognising the benefits to businesses of people being able to travel to a meeting in London and back inside a day, the authorities at JFK Airport did eventually allow Concorde landing rights in 1979. However, by this stage further development of the project had been scrapped and the capacity to build more of the aircraft had been crippled. The record crossing between London Heathrow and New York JFK was 2 hours 52 minutes – less than half the time a Boeing 747 would take to make the same journey. Interestingly the subsonic record for crossing the Atlantic is held by another British built airliner, the VC-10, at just 5 hours and 1 minute. This has been beaten by two Boeing aircraft but only with the assistance of natural phenomena.

The Concorde fleet flew until 2003. It had a 16-month sabbatical after the crash of Flight 4590 at Charles De Gaulle Airport, Paris, in 2000. This was the only fatal accident involving any of the Concorde fleet. It was not caused by any fault of the aircraft. A piece of debris on the runway had not been cleared by the airport authorities and this was catapulted by the undercarriage into the fuel tank of the Concorde. The resulting explosion killed the 109 people on board. Work was undertaken to strengthen the casing of the fuel tanks by lining them with Kevlar – a bullet and knife resistant material used by police and armed forces. The additional weight had to be compensated by replacing all the seats inside the cabin.

Concorde returned to the skies in November 2001 but passenger numbers were vastly reduced, partly because of the crash in 2000, but more so because the 11th September 2001 terrorist attacks in the United States had caused a drop in air travel throughout the world. Due to this decline in passenger numbers, both Air France and British Airways simultaneously announced in 2003 that their Concorde fleet would be retired in July of that year. The very last Concorde to fly, G-BOAF, is housed in the Bristol Aerospace Museum that is signposted off the A38. Visitors can step aboard the aircraft and admire plenty of other aircraft and components on display.

Bristol City Centre has a lot to offer and is well worth staying in for a couple of days. The city's wealth and history are founded on its trade, particularly with North America. In fact, the first European to discover mainland North America was John Cabot, a Venetian who sailed out of Bristol on an expedition commissioned by Henry VII. The newest section of the city's retail centre is named Cabot Circus in his honour.

Being on the western side of England it is well positioned for the export of goods that over the centuries have been brought to Bristol by canal, rail and road as well as the import of goods from overseas. Bristol was one of the global trading hubs at the height of the British Empire, being a short journey up the Avon from the Bristol Channel and the Atlantic. As cargo vessels grew in both size and their water displacement, the docks in the centre of the city became less suitable and were moved out to Avonmouth (see section on Junction 18). The city is not without controversy. It is estimated that over two thousand Bristol-registered ships were involved in the slave trade during the 18th Century, transporting over 500,000 Africans to North America and trading them for produce such as tobacco, sugar, tropical fruit and tea leaves which would be sailed back into Bristol. The slave trade continued to haunt Bristol in June 2020 during the 'Black Lives Matters' protests that were taking place around the world at the time. A statue of Edward Colston was torn down by protestors and dropped in the river. Colston was one of the city's former merchant, philanthropist and Member of Parliament who profited from the slave trade.

SS Great Britain

An excellent museum dedicated to Bristol's trading heritage is located on the south side of the docks at the SS Great Britain. Visitors can board the preserved vessel, walk all around her and even walk beneath her to admire the hull and propellers. Designed by Isambard Kingdom Brunel, the SS Great Britain was built in Bristol and launched in 1843. She was the first vessel to combine a steam-driven screw propeller with an iron hull that would be the basis for all ships built from then on. Built for luxury Trans-Atlantic passenger travel, she revolutionised international travel. The vessel was operated by the Great Western Steamship Company – a sister company to the Great Western Railway of which Brunel had famously been the Chief Architect and Engineer.

In a similar manner to Concorde, the SS Great Britain became a commercial failure very quickly. Due in no small part to Brunel's input, the building of iron-hulled vessels increased, and steam engine-driven propeller technology developed very quickly in terms of efficiency. By 1850, the SS Great Britain was very expensive to run compared to vessels that were only a few years younger. Indeed, the Great Western Steamship Company had gone out of business in 1846 because of the expense of the vessel. The vessel then had several subsequent owners and upon the establishment of gold mines in Australia she was briefly used for transporting migrants there.

Revolution in more ways than one SS Great Britain

By 1882 she was converted to a sailing vessel and in 1886 suffered a fire whilst in the South Atlantic that damaged her beyond economic repair. The vessel was then used as a floating coal bunker in the Falkland Islands until she was scuttled in 1937. In the late 1960s a private consortium planned and funded the raising of the SS Great Britain in 1970. The vessel was towed back to where she was built, in the Great Western Dock, Bristol. The SS Great Britain underwent decades of careful restoration and it was completed in 2005 and the site is one of the finest restorations of a historic engineering project anywhere in the world.

Not far from Bristol's waterfront is Temple Meads Railway station. Opened as part of the Great Western Railway, it is another fine example of Brunel's work. The facade of the railway station is exquisitely ornate and if the railway signs were removed, visitors could be forgiven for mistaking the building for a palace.

Brunel's mark on Bristol did not end with the railway and the SS Great Britain, it also has one of the most famous bridges in Europe. The Clifton Suspension Bridge links the Bristolian suburb of Clifton with Leigh Woods in North Somerset. A bridge over the Avon gorge was a huge engineering challenge due to several factors. Firstly, the Admiralty had legislated in the mid-18th Century that any bridge built over the Avon Gorge must leave a clearance of at least 100ft for tall masted vessels to sail in and out of Bristol Docks. Secondly, the tide from the Bristol Channel contributed to the clearance. Thirdly, the span required was in excess of 700ft. Work on constructing the bridge began in the 1830s but was held up several times by riots in the city and funding blockages – including a period of 10 years where no work was done on the project. Brunel died in 1859 and his colleagues William Barlow and John Hawkshaw were determined to finish the bridge as a memorial to the great man. The Clifton Suspension Bridge was opened in 1864 and is an impressive 245ft above the Avon at high tide. A toll is still payable to cross it to this day.

Clifton Suspension Bridge

Bristol is also credited to be the birthplace of the Methodist Church as it is where John Wesley established the first Methodist Chapel at the New Room on Broadmead in 1739. Prior to having the New Room built, John Wesley and his brother, Charles, would preach in the open air to crowds in the city centre. The New Room is open to the public and there are services and other events held there on a regular basis.

There are two football clubs in the city: Bristol Rovers and Bristol City. Rovers play home matches at the Memorial Ground, built in 1921 in memory of Rugby Union players who were killed during the Great War. The Memorial Ground was a dual-purpose stadium until 2014, with Bristol Bears Rugby Club also playing home matches there until they moved across the city to groundshare with Bristol City at Ashton Gate. Rovers currently play in the third tier of English football and have never played above the second tier. Bristol City currently play in the second tier and last played in the topflight between 1976 and 1980. Bristol Bears have had mixed fortunes of late, fluctuating between Premiership Rugby and its second tier.

Junction 17: Cribbs Causeway

A junction to be avoided during the last few weekends before Christmas, the first site immediately off the junction is the Mall at Cribbs Causeway, an enclosed shopping centre with over 130 stores. The name 'Cribbs Causeway' is supposedly the name of the route between the centre of Bristol and the village of Aust where the ferry across the Severn Estuary could be boarded.

Motorists can drive directly from the M5 to Clifton via the A4018 leading directly into the suburb. As well as the suspension bridge, Clifton boasts many acres of open space at Clifton Downs. The views across the gorge into North Somerset as well as of the bridge itself make for beautiful scenic walks and picnic areas. Perfect for a lunch stop to break up a long journey on the M5.

On a clear day, motorists can see across to the Severn Bridge and Chepstow whilst travelling between Junctions 16 and 17.

Junction 18: Avonmouth

After Junction 17, motorists descend a long hill towards Avonmouth. The views across it will leave travellers with no doubt that this is the modern industrial and trading area of Bristol. As the size of vessels grew during the 19th Century, ports like those in the centre of Bristol became less suitable. In 1860 work began on a landing stage at the 'Avon's Mouth'. By 1865 a railway station and pier had been constructed and the station was named 'Avonmouth', giving the area its name. Originally in Gloucestershire, the county boundary was moved in 1894 so that Avonmouth transferred to the control of the City of Bristol. Various expansions to Avonmouth Docks occurred into the beginning of the 20th Century. The Royal Edward dock was built during the reign of Edward VII and was further expanded in the 1920s.

Avonmouth is one of the primary ports in Britain for the import of refrigerated products. Particularly tropical and 'out of season' fruit and vegetables. This is a continuation of what Bristol used to import from North America from the 16th Century onwards. Avonmouth was also a terminal at one time for coal and steel being brought a short distance by barges from South Wales for distribution by rail to the rest of England.

Aside from the port, Avonmouth's rise as an industrial area began during the First World War when the primary facility of the National Smelting Company (NSC) was built in nearby Chittening to provide munitions for the military, particularly mustard gas shells. By the end of the war, over 80,000 mustard gas shells were produced at the NSC, by the mostly female workforce. There were over 150 reported accidents in the factory and over 1,000 recorded burns.

Following a Defence Review in the 1970s, NSC ceased production of munitions at Chittening but the site continued to be used for stockpiling of weaponry until it closed in the early 2000s. It is now owned by the supermarket chain ASDA, who use it as a distribution centre for imported goods. In addition to ASDA there are dozens of companies that have distribution centres in the vicinity of Avonmouth, including Royal Mail, DHL, DSV, Honda and Accolade Wines. The 'multi-channel' retailer, The Range, also has a distribution centre in Avonmouth. The building covers 55 acres of land and is, therefore, the largest single-footprint warehouse in Britain.

The westernmost end of the A4 connects Avonmouth with the centre of Bristol. Traditionally known as the Bath Road, the A4's eastern terminus begins in Westminster. The six-mile stretch of the A4 between Avonmouth and Bristol City centre follows the Avon and passes underneath the Clifton Suspension Bridge, spanning across the gorge some 230ft above the road. This is the most direct route from the M5 to the SS Great Britain museum.

Continuing along the motorway after Junction 18 takes motorists immediately on to the Avonmouth Bridge, the second time the M5 crosses a river named Avon. The M5 was built as far as Avonmouth docks in 1970 however the Avonmouth Bridge was not completed until 1974, when the M5 extended into Somerset and continued towards the sections being built on the route into Devon. The total length of the bridge is 0.875 miles and the centre of its span has a clearance of 100ft above the Avon at high tide. Although originally built with three lanes on each carriageway, the Avonmouth Bridge was reconfigured in the early 2000s to four lane traffic in each direction.

When travelling across the bridge, motorists can get a sense of the tidal effect of the Bristol Channel. At low tide, the banks of the Avon are extremely steep and treacherously muddy. At high tide, the river appears somewhat bloated. Looking westwards there are views across Royal Portbury Dock and, on clear days, across the Bristol Channel towards the city of Newport.

Portishead

Junction 19: Royal Portbury Docks & Portishead

The far left lane heading southbound on the Avonmouth Bridge filters traffic to exit at Junction 19 at Easton-in-Gordano. Gordano Services is often one of the busiest on the M5 as it serves both carriageways and it is the first services on the M5 after the interchange with the M4. Consequently, it has a wider choice of food and drink outlets.

Constructed between 1972 and 1977 Royal Portbury Docks are the newest addition to the Port of Bristol. The primary export from Portbury is motor vehicles, with up to 650,000 British built vehicles being exported out of Portbury each year. The docks have capacity for up to 6 'roll on/roll off' vessels to be docked simultaneously to handle this aspect of international trade. There are also two large cranes for loading and unloading containers. Between them, they can handle 5,000 tonnes of cargo per hour.

Portbury has links with the aviation industry. Components that are manufactured in Filton and other locations in Gloucestershire are loaded on to ships at Portbury. One example is the wings of the Airbus A400M

Atlas, which were loaded on to specialised ferries to take them for assembly in Seville. When Portbury first opened in the late 1970s, one of the continuous imports was coal mined overseas. Trains would take the coal from the docks to Didcot Power Station. The mounds of stockpiled coal were a common sight for motorists crossing the Avonmouth Bridge until the late 2010s when coal-fired electricity generation was beginning to be phased out.

The town of Portishead was also part of the Port of Bristol until 1992. The former dock has been redeveloped as a marina with the surrounding land regenerated in the style of a Cornish fishing village. The developers claim that Portishead Marina is modelled on Polperro with coloured houses and shops and narrow pedestrianised streets. There used to be two coal and oil-fired power stations alongside the former dock, but these were demolished to make way for the more colourful urban centre that visitors see today. Portishead has a link with the northern tip of the M5 as its lighthouse was built by the Chance Brothers of Smethwick.

Portishead was also played a valuable role during the Second World War as a primary radio-station for shore to ship transmissions. The radio communications were one way because the warships were ordered not to reply – to do so would risk revealing their position to the enemy. After the war the station was one of the largest broadcasters of maritime and aeronautical radio communications in the world until its closure in 2000, the increased use of satellite communications having led to a decline in the use of radio signals.

Junctions 19–20: The Gordano Valley

After Junction 19, the M5 ascends in altitude to overlook the Gordano Valley to the west. The valley does not have a river, it is mainly land reclaimed from the Bristol Channel now having an agricultural use. The southbound and northbound carriageways split here with southbound being around 25ft above the northbound side.

On a clear day, motorists travelling southbound can overlook the villages of Walton-in-Gordano and Weston-in-Gordano and see through a gap in the hills towards Cardiff and Penarth. As the carriageway then starts to descend towards Junction 20, motorists get a view across Clevedon, Wick St Lawrence and Sand Point peninsular. This is also motorists' last view of the sea on the M5 until its end.

The northbound journey between Junctions 20 and 19 is spectacular on a clear day. Once above the Gordano Valley, motorists will be able to see a stunning vista of the Severn Estuary including both Severn Bridges, Royal Portbury and Avonmouth docks, Chepstow and, in the distance, the hills of the Royal Forest of Dean. On a clear day this is one of the most comprehensive and stunning views on any motorway throughout Europe.

Less than a mile from Junction 20, the M5 passes the grounds of Clevedon Court, a 14th Century stately home. Although it is now owned by the National Trust, it has been occupied by the Elton family since the 18th Century, the first occupant from the family being the Sheriff of Bristol. The Eltons, being a wealthy and influential family used to invite several prominent literary authors to stay at Clevedon Court as their guests as they would have been the celebrities of their times. The authors included William Thackeray, Alfred Tennyson, Samuel Taylor Coleridge and the Bronte Sisters.

Clevedon

Junction 20: Clevedon & Nailsea

Away from the built-up areas around Bristol, Avonmouth and Portbury, Junction 20 delivers motorists into the rural area of North Somerset. If it were not for the M5, a complex series of country lanes would need to be travelled to get motorists from Bristol to Clevedon. When there are incidents closing or causing congestion on the M5 in the Avonmouth area, the resulting tailbacks can be huge due to the roads and lanes in North Somerset being unsuitable for large volumes of traffic.

The coastal town of Clevedon is a great place to stop off for lunch to break up a lengthy journey on the M5. It retains its Victorian character, having benefited greatly during the 18th and 19th Centuries from the benevolence of the Elton family at Clevedon Court. Perhaps the most prominent and long-lasting contribution to the town is the clock standing at the centre of the main shopping area. The Curzon Cinema opened in the town centre in 1912 and is now the world's oldest cinema in continuous operation.

The sea front is around half a mile from the town centre and aside from the motor vehicles that can park on the street, it is difficult to imagine it having looked any different 150 years ago. The pier opened in 1869 to facilitate the coastal steamers operating in the Bristol Channel and beyond. Although these services are a fraction of the scale they used to be, the Waverley and the MV Balmoral do still dock at Clevedon to embark and disembark passengers from time to time. There are various levels of the pier so that vessels can dock and embark passengers without being disrupted by the 49ft tidal range in the Bristol Channel.

Aside from the pier's function as a jetty for vessels, it serves only one other purpose: a pleasant place to stroll and take in views of the estuary. At the far end of the pier, pedestrians can view part of the span of the Second Severn Crossing. A few minutes' pleasant walk south along the promenade will take visitors to Salthouse Fields, an open space featuring a 'ride on' miniature railway. Adjacent to Salthouse Fields is Clevedon Marine Lake whose water is replenished daily by the high tide. It is very popular with children who like to go 'crabbing' and exploring any other marine life that may have been left by the tide.

Clevedon has influenced the pharmaceutical industry, being the first place where penicillin was produced on an industrial scale. In 1938 scientist Alexander Fleming wrote a paper about the antibacterial properties of Penicillium notatum mould. Within a few months the Admiralty arranged for this to be explored further by their Antibiotic Research team at the Royal Navy Medical School in Clevedon during the late 1930s and early 1940s.

Junction 20 also serves Nailsea, a traditional mining town. The nearby Elms Colliery is one of the most complete examples of an 18th Century colliery in England and is now a scheduled ancient monument. Glassblowing also used to take place in Nailsea. The Glassworks were bought by the Chance Brothers of Smethwick in 1870 to produce a decorative style of glass but they closed the factory after three years as the supply of local coal ran out. Nailsea glass is a sought-after collector's item nowadays. There is a sculpture of a glassblower near the site of the former glassworks in the town.

Junction 21: Weston-Super-Mare

The main purpose of this junction is to serve the large seaside town of Weston-Super-Mare, known more simply as 'Weston'. Junction 21 links the M5 to the A370, a trunk road between Bristol and East Brent that also flows through Weston. Driving northeast on the A370 towards Congresbury takes motorists to Puxton Park, a working farm and family activity park. It provides a wonderful opportunity for visitors to learn about the agricultural industry and has a wide range of activities and rides for children of all ages to enjoy. There is also a large indoor soft play centre, providing a useful Plan B during poor weather and featuring a vertical drop slide that can be enjoyed by adults too. Admission is not payable for visitors who only want to use the café and farm shop which stocks a variety of produce of the farm and from the rest of Somerset, making it a useful stop off for lunch a couple of minutes' drive from the M5.

Weston-Super-Mare is a large town on the shores of the Bristol Channel. Like many seaside towns, there was very little of note in the area until the advent of the railways and the introduction of labour laws during the 19th Century. Labour laws allowed workers days off as well as holiday leave and rail travel meant that the populations of cities could journey to the seaside faster and cheaper than before, opening the tourism economy to the working class for the first time. The population of Bristol could journey to Weston and back in a day. Populations of landlocked cities such as Birmingham and Coventry could journey to the seaside within a few hours – making a short holiday feasible and affordable.

Isambard Kingdom Brunel lived in Weston with his family whilst he was supervising the construction of the Bristol-Exeter Railway that made such journeys possible. Part of that line passes through Bleadon Hill, a couple of miles south of Weston. A gorge was cut into the hill to allow the line to pass through. Pre-existing roads were then reconnected with bridges. The bridge carrying the eponymous Bleadon Hill was the highest single span bridge over a railway line in the country when it opened.

Within a few years of the arrival of the railway, towns like Weston were growing and adapting to serve the newfound tourist industry. Guesthouses and holiday camps were built. Amusements and activities were arranged for the visitors and, two centuries later, are something of a tradition. In Weston, the two oldest, and arguably most famous, activities are the traditional donkey rides on the beach and the two piers. Now derelict, Birnbeck Pier opened in 1867 to facilitate coastal steamers docking in the town that ferried visitors from the mining communities of South Wales. It has the distinction of being the only pier in Britain that connects the mainland to an island – Birnbeck Island. The Grand Pier opened in Weston in 1904 and is the epicentre for the visitors' attractions in the town. At over 1,200ft long it is not a short pier, however the height of the tide in the Bristol Channel can mean that at low-tide, the pier is entirely above sand, as the sea can be up to a mile from the promenade. It is often joked that people go to Weston for the day but never see the sea!

More recent additions to Weston's range of attractions include the Seaquarium, Funland Tropicana, Weston Carnival Sand Sculptures, a 130ft Ferris wheel, the Winter Gardens and a dotto train. All of them are on the seafront. The Winter Gardens deserves a special mention as it has been a multi-use venue since its construction in the 1920s. During the 1960s and 1970s it hosted music concerts performed by Pink Floyd, Cilla Black, David Bowie, Deep Purple, Slade and T Rex. It is now owned by the local college. Weston is also the final stage on the West Country Carnival route. The illuminated procession takes place on several days every autumn and dates back to the Gunpowder Plot of 1603. This event has the main purpose of raising money for local charities however it also benefits the local economy by attracting visitors outside the peak holiday season.

Further inland is the Helicopter Museum. It is clearly signposted off the A370 and contains a collection of helicopters and gyrocopters from around the world. The museum's origins date back to the late 1950s when aviation historian and author, Elfan Ap Rees, began collecting rotary aircraft that were either surplus or beyond repair. His collection grew over three decades and in 1989 the collection was converted into a museum and was opened to the public. The Helicopter Museum now has over 80 aircraft on static display and several more under restoration. It is on the site of a former airfield, RAF Weston-Super-Mare. Originally a training school for the Royal Air Force when it opened in 1936, between 1944 and 1946 it was used to train Polish fighter pilots. It was then used as a helicopter supply station until 1987.

Two television personalities were born in Weston-Super-Mare: John Cleese in 1939 and Jill Dando in 1961. Cleese is a comic actor who is most famous for his roles in Monty Python and Fawlty Towers as well as being an 'apprentice' to Q in two James Bond films. Jill Dando was a journalist who began her career at *The Weston Mercury* newspaper in 1980. She started work as a presenter on BBC Radio Devon in 1985 and then transferred to television journalism within a couple of years. Dando is perhaps best remembered for hosting the BBC programmes 'Holiday' and 'Crimewatch' as well as occasional episodes of 'Songs of Praise'. Tragically, Jill Dando was murdered outside her London home in 1999. Although an individual named Barry George was convicted of her murder, he was latterly acquitted and no one else has been charged with her murder. In the town's Grove Park there is a memorial garden dedicated to her. It was constructed by hosts of the BBC's 'Ground Force' series as well as family members, friends and former colleagues from *The Weston Mercury*.

Jill Dando Memorial Garden

The islands of Flat Holm and Steep Holm can be seen clearly from Weston's seafront. Flat Holm is a Welsh Island and is currently leased as a nature reserve by Cardiff City Council. After the Norman invasion of England in 1066, the island was a temporary refuge for Gytha Thorkelsdottir, mother of the last Anglo-Saxon King of England, Harold II. In more recent centuries, Flat Holm has been frequented by smugglers for hiding tobacco, brandy and other products from the Customs & Excise Officers in the Ports of Cardiff and Bristol. Flat Holm was also the base from where the first radio signal was transmitted across water in 1897. Guglielmo Marconi sent the words 'are you ready?' in Morse Code to a receiving tower near Penarth.

Steep Holm is in 'English Waters' and rises to 200ft above the Bristol Channel. It was fortified during the 1860s in anticipation of an attempted invasion by the French. Further military hardware was added between 1914 and 1918, primarily to protect Bristol and Cardiff against attempted enemy incursions. It was staffed by the Indian Army Service Corps. This operation was resumed during the Second World War. Steep Holm is now largely a nature reserve owned by the Memorial Trust of Kenneth Allsop, an author and nature expert for BBC Television in the 1960s.

Junctions 21 to 22: Sedgemoor

This stretch of motorway is characteristically very flat, traversing the Somerset Levels, large portions being reclaimed land. The M5 crosses a number of watercourses, namely the River Banwell, the Lox Yeo River and the River Axe. All these eventually culminate in the Bristol Channel and, as with the two Avons and the Severn, the high tide is a dangerous catalyst for widespread flooding on the Somerset Levels after periods of heavy rainfall. Most of the watercourses have had sluice-gates installed to mitigate the tidal impact during conventional periods of weather. This is not so much to protect homes and buildings, but to minimise disruption to the agricultural industry that is the lifeblood of Somerset.

The Battle of Sedgemoor took place on the Somerset Levels on 6th July 1685. It was the final battle of the Monmouth Rebellion, an insurrection against James II of England (VII of Scotland) led by his nephew, James Scott. James II had ascended to the British throne after his brother, Charles II, died with no legitimate children to inherit the crown. Historians claim that Charles II fathered 14 children outside of his marriage to Catherine of Braganza, however James Scott claimed that his mother, Lucy Walter, married his father in a secret ceremony whilst he was Prince of Wales.

Charles II died on 6th February 1685 and the Duke of Monmouth lived in the Netherlands at the time, commanding joint Anglo-Dutch military units in the aftermath of the English Civil War. His ambition to ascend to the British throne was stoked up when his Catholic uncle was named King. Believing he could rally the mainly Protestant English, he sailed to Lyme Regis in June of that year and very quickly began to raise support throughout the West Country – a historically rebellious region of England.

The rebels were decisively beaten near the village of Westonzoyland to the east of Bridgwater, however the name of the battle, Sedgemoor, encompasses 217 square miles of the Somerset Levels where the battle took place. One of the leaders of the King's forces that defeated them was John Churchill, the First Duke of Marlborough and an ancestor of Sir Winston Churchill. Those rebels who were not killed during the battle were able to flee but were subsequently hunted down and arrested by the King's troops. They were tried by the King's Chief Prosecutor, Judge Jeffries, at various locations throughout the West Country in what have become known as the Bloody Assizes. The rebels on trial either faced deportation to the colonies for a term of hard labour or they were hanged, drawn and quartered.

James Scott was arrested two days after the Battle of Sedgemoor and was beheaded a further seven days later. James II was eventually deposed three years later during the Glorious Revolution, replaced by his daughter, Mary II, and her husband William of Orange. At this point, the prosecutor Judge Jefferies was also arrested and held in the Tower of London where he was reported to have died of alcoholism.

Junction 22: Burnham-on-Sea, Highbridge & the Brean Peninsular

Burnham-on-Sea is a 'quiet neighbour' of Weston-Super-Mare, although the town can be very busy itself in the peak holiday season. Forming a single parish, Highbridge and Burnham share a population that is a quarter of that of Weston, but both are much older. The name 'Burnham' is derived from 'hemm' meaning enclosed. The reason being much of the land to the east of Burnham is reclaimed from the sea. At high tide, the medieval community in Burnham could be completely cut off. The town is vulnerable to flooding from ferocious weather on the Bristol Channel but this threat has been mitigated by a wave return wall that was built along the sea front during the late 1980s. It was the largest of its kind at the time.

Due to the treacherous sailing conditions in the Bristol Channel, Burnham was the site of three lighthouses positioned to warn ships of the risk of running aground on the continuously shifting sands. Only one, the Low Lighthouse, is still operational and it is a unique looking construction built on the beach. It is known informally as the lighthouse on legs. The first lighthouse in the town was a beacon that was lit above St Andrew's Church. The church is now worth a visit as the tower is leaning due to poor foundations. The top of the tower is 3 feet further north than its base.

Due to the treacherous prevailing sands in this part of the Bristol Channel, the Burnham rescue boat is a hovercraft housed at the southern end of the town. It is funded as a charity and is operated independently of the Royal National Lifeboat Institute, although it can be called to action by the Coastguard in exactly the same manner as the RNLI.

Views across the Bridgwater Bay area and the wider Bristol Channel can be enjoyed from Burnham seafront. A feature of the western side of Bridgewater Bay is Hinkley Point, the location of three nuclear power stations. Hinkley Point A went online in 1957 and was decommissioned in 2000. Hinkley Point B was commissioned in 1967 and is due to end production of electricity in the mid-2020s. The third Hinkley Point power station is currently under construction and is due to be commissioned in 2025. Part of the construction of the new reactor includes a concrete base measuring at 9,000 square metres, the largest pouring of concrete in history. This base is reinforced by 5,000 tonnes of Welsh steel and is to protect the environment in the event of a reactor meltdown.

There are numerous holiday parks and campsites throughout Burnham and Brean, an extension of sorts to the popularity of Weston, but also a testament to the attractiveness of this part of Somerset and the relative ease of holidaying in the area thanks to the M5.

Although the village of Brean is only a couple of miles from Weston, they are separated by the estuary of the River Axe. The name of the village is derived from the Welsh word 'bryn' translating as 'hill'. The hill known as Brean Down is on a peninsula to the west of the Axe. It is largely a nature reserve enjoyed by bird watchers, walkers and cyclists. There is a fortification on the western tip of the peninsula which, along with those of Flat Holm and Steep Holm, was built to defend against an anticipated French invasion during the 1860s. The sandy beach at Brean is open to motorists at non-peak times. This allows for an enjoyable picnic spot where food does not need to be taken far from the car.

Highbridge is located at the estuary of the River Brue and contained a small wharf until the early 20th Century benefiting the town's livestock and cheese market as well as Buncombes, a local steam roller manufacturer. Eventually the wharf became redundant due to the growing size of newer vessels. Neither Buncombe nor the market exist now and so aside from retail employment and caravan dealers, Highbridge primarily serves as a dormitory town.

Junction 22 is also a convenient exit for Cheddar, a village noted for lending its name to a cheese recipe and for the stunning limestone gorge and caves that were formed during the ice age. The most famous set of caves is The Wookey Hole, six miles south of the village. Cheddar can be reached by following the A38 in a northerly direction and turning towards the A371 at Axbridge, it is clearly signposted. If motorists are heading to Cheddar from the north, the full length of the gorge can be enjoyed by journeying via M32 into the centre of Bristol, following the A37 towards Farrington Gurney, then the A39 towards Green Ore and then the B3135, leading directly into the centre of the village.

Cheddar is a busy place in peak holiday season, and it attracts half a million visitors per year. Although Cheddar Cheese is the most popular in Britain, there is only one small-scale producer of it in the village. Its name is not protected by law in the same way that Champagne and Melton Mowbray Pork Pies are. Yeo Valley, one of Britain's largest producers of dairy foods, has a large facility just outside Cheddar, and its company headquarters is in Blagdon, a village on the opposite side of the Mendip Hills.

Continuing along the M5 from Junction 22, motorists should be able to see the Quantock Hills to the west. The range of continues along the Somerset coast into the Exmoor National Park. Heading towards Junction 23, the M5 crosses the Rivers Brue and Huntspill. The sluice gates installed to control the tidal impact can be seen from the carriageway. On very clear days, it is also possible to see across to Glastonbury Tor.

Wells

Junctions 23 & 24: The A39, Bridgewater, Minehead, Street, Glastonbury & Wells.

Bridgewater is a town that has historically grown around its modest port and the crossroads of what is now the A38 and A39. A junction between north, south, east and west, the sea, and a stopping point for travellers between the Mendip and Quantock Hills as well as a crossing over the River Parrett. In 1785, Bridgewater was the first town to petition Parliament to abolish slavery.

One of the most influential residents of Bridgewater was Robert Blake, to whom there is a statue and a museum dedicated in the town. Blake is considered by many historians to be the father of the Royal Navy. He was appointed General at Sea in 1649, the rank of Admiral was not used whilst England was under Parliamentary control during the Civil War. In 1651 he published the first set of printed rules for the Royal Navy, entitled The Laws of War and Ordinances of the Sea. It contained regulations for everything including attack and blockade tactics through to court martials and their appropriate punishments. He also instigated a policy of having an armed fleet at sea all year round, rather than during the fairer weather months as had been the case prior to his command. As with all civil wars, foreign powers tried to take advantage of Britain's internal strife by trying to gain a foothold on its colonies and outlying British isles. The navies of Spain, Portugal, the Netherlands and the Rhineland were all seen off by the fleets under Blake's command.

Some recently built landmarks in Bridgewater are seen directly from the M5 between Junctions 23 and 24. The supermarket chain Morrisons has its regional distribution centre for the southwest adjacent to the M5. The 192-acre site provides stock for 65 stores in the region. The adjacent plot of land is a residential estate built during the late 1990s and early 2000s. A unique feature of the estate is Willow Man, a celebration of the widespread use of willow on the Somerset Levels. The 40ft sculpture is the second to be built on the site as the first was burnt down by arsonists in 2000. The current sculpture has a moat dug around it to discourage a second arson attack.

At Junction 23 the M5 is crossed by the former national trunk road, the A39. Once known as the Atlantic Highway, it connects Bath with Falmouth, following the coast of Somerset, North Devon and North Cornwall before turning towards the south coast for its last stage. Turning west on the A39 will take motorists beyond Bridgwater and Hinkley Point towards Dunster and Minehead.

Dunster is a medieval town and the main street has not altered for four centuries. The focal point of the town is the Yarn Market dating back to 1647 and is now a listed monument. Dunster Castle is on the site of a Norman fort that overlooks the town and Blue Anchor Bay. It is built from sandstone making its red expanse an impressive sight as motorists approach the town on the A39. It was owned by the Luttrell family from the 14th Century until 1976 when it was given to the National Trust. During December the town hosts a candlelit fare that features a procession of flaming torches.

Dunster

Two miles west of Dunster is the seaside town of Minehead. It is a popular destination for visitors due to its attractive location and being the western terminus of the West Somerset Railway. Formerly the Minehead Railway, it was closed in 1971 following the Beaching Report. In 1976 it reopened as a heritage railway, the longest one in England. Butlins opened one of its holiday camps in Minehead in 1961 and remains the largest provider of accommodation in the town. This can mean that the A39 is extremely busy between Bridgewater and Minehead on Fridays: changeover day for campers. Minehead is also the hometown of science fiction writer, Arthur C Clarke.

Further west of Minehead, the A39 passes through the village of Porlock, and immediately ascends on to Exmoor. Featuring several hairpin bends and gradients of 1 in 4 (25%), the road climbs 1,300 feet in less than two miles making it the steepest A-class road in Britain. It is common to smell tired brakes and clutches of vehicles passing through Porlock.

Turning east on the A39 from Junction 23 takes motorists towards Street, a small industrial town that traditionally manufactured shoes. Hush Puppies and Clarks were the dominant shoemakers in the town before their manufacturing divisions were transferred overseas. Clarks still retains a presence in the town, converting part of its former factory into a shopping outlet with a focus on footwear. The firm's primary distribution centre also remains amongst the Clarks estate.

A short journey north of Street is the town of Glastonbury, a town that predates the Norman invasion of 1066, with a Saxon Abbey being founded in the town during the 7th Century. The centre certainly has a new age feel, with independent shops selling crystals, curios, spiritual books and a whole range of items that would appeal to 'hippies'.

It is the two features outside the town that perhaps make Glastonbury famous. Firstly, over a mile to the east of the town is Glastonbury Tor. Visible for miles in all directions, it is a hilltop ruin of St Michael's Church and only the tower remains. It has been the focus of myths and legends down the centuries as it is said to be Avalon, the legendary place where King Arthur's sword was forged. Glastonbury Tor is also considered to be a possible location of the Holy Grail. Whether or not people believe these legends to have any truth, it is undisputedly a beautiful location. Glastonbury Tor attracts tens of thousands of visitors per year and it is now owned by the National Trust.

The other outside feature that brings the town fame is the Glastonbury Festival. Taking place in the village of Pilton, almost six miles to the east, the festival is a celebration of music and arts that takes place four out of every five years. The festival attracts around 200,000 people, most of whom bring tents to sleep in for the five days. The campers' resolve can often be tested as it is rare for a festival to take place without at least one deluge. As well as contemporary musicians, comedians, poets and actors perform at Glastonbury Festival.

Continuing northeast on the A39 takes motorists to Wells, England's smallest city. The impressive Cathedral Church of St Andrew was built in stages between the 12th and 15th Centuries but was not designated as a Cathedral until 1953 after a reorganisation of the diocese. Inside, there is an astronomical clock displaying the position of Earth and the sun, the phases of the moon and the 24 hours of the day. Upon the hour, jousting knights chase each other around the top of the clock. Associated with the Cathedral is Wells Cathedral School, founded in 909. It is one of only five independent coeducational schools in England that has a primary focus on music.

The City Centre is very compact, but pedestrians must be wary of the cobbled streets as well as the water-gullies running between the road and the pavements carrying a stream towards the nearby River Sheppey. The Bishop's Palace in the west of the city has been the official residence of the Bishops of the Diocese of Bath and Wells for 800 years and is well worth a walk to see the classic moat and draw bridge. There is a good mix of independent and chain retailers as well as places to get refreshments. Wells is a must-visit place on the edge of the Mendip Hills.

Taunton Castle

Junction 25: Taunton & West Dorset

Taunton became the County Town of Somerset in the early 14th Century, taking over the role from the geographically remote town of Somerton. The name of the town has evolved down the centuries from 'Town on the Tone'. The River Tone, a tributary of the River Parrett, meanders through the centre of the town. Motorists can see Taunton's most distinctive landmark from the M5, the 111ft tower of St James's Church. The medieval church is adjacent to the County Ground, home of Somerset County Cricket Club.

On 20th June 1685, the Duke of Monmouth 'crowned' himself King of England in Taunton. Within a few weeks of his defeat, Taunton Castle hosted one of the Bloody Assizes overseen by Judge Jefferies. The castle is now the Museum of Somerset, a few yards from the town's retail centre. It has plenty of places to get lunch or afternoon tea. To the south of the town is Vivary Park, where Taunton Flower Festival has been held every August since 1866, apart from during years of national crises. The event

74

attracts some 17,000 visitors per year and is described as the 'Chelsea of the West'.

The Ministry of Defence has a presence in Taunton with 40 Commando Royal Marines being based in the town. The United Kingdom Hydrographic Office is also based in the town. A trading arm of the Ministry of Defence, the UKHO provides marine navigation, weather reports and geospatial information to shipping companies throughout the world.

The Bridgwater and Taunton Canal was part of an aborted scheme to create a waterway between the Bristol Channel and the English Channel during the 18th and 19th Centuries. In more recent history, the canal formed part of the 'Taunton Stop Line' during the Second World War. This was a defensive position organised by the Ministry of War to defend against a German invasion force that could feasibly land in remote parts of Devon and Cornwall and advance east. The line extends 50 miles south towards Axminster in Devon. There are still some pillboxes along the canal, their presence can be surprising this far inland to those unaware of their history.

Junction 25 is also clearly signposted as the exit from the M5 for journeys to Yeovil, Weymouth and Dorchester from the north. Experienced drivers would not use this exit, however, as the A358 towards the A303 can get very congested. A less congested, and more scenic, route would be to leave the M5 at Junction 23 and head towards Street on the A39, then Somerton and Ilchester on the B3151 and Yeovil on the A37. Weymouth, Dorchester and other destinations in West Dorset can then be reached by following the A37 south out of Yeovil.

Another destination signposted at Junction 25, is the Fleet Air Arm Museum, but again it is advisable to use the directions above. The museum is aside the Royal Naval Air Station at Yeovilton, an operational base primarily supporting and maintaining the helicopters of the Royal Navy. Fighter pilots of the Fleet Air Arm also undergo training there. The museum contains a fine collection of historic helicopters, fighters and other aircraft. This includes a connection along the M5 to Filton as one of the prototype Concordes, G-BSST, is on display and can be boarded. Visitors can also walk around a mock-up of part of the flight deck of one of the former British aircraft carriers, HMS Ark Royal.

Junction 26: Wellington & the Blackdown Hills

Junctions 25 to 29 is perhaps the sparsest section of the M5, motorists cannot see much of Wellington from the M5 because it is shielded by trees and farmland, but they can see the Wellington Monument to the east of the motorway. Situated on the northern slopes of the Blackdown Hills, the 175ft obelisk is a memorial to the Duke of Wellington. Born in Dublin, Arthur Wellesley was an officer in the British Army and was offered a peerage after his victory at the Battle of Talavera in 1809. As the name of the town sounded close to his family name, and there was a local manor yet to be taken, he chose the title of Duke of Wellington. Of course, he is best remembered for commanding the allied forces against Napoleon at the Battle of Waterloo in 1815. The monument was originally intended to be a celebration of the victory, but the Duke died before it was completed. There are a number of towns and cities throughout the world named Wellington, usually in honour of the Duke. The most notable example is New Zealand's capital.

Wellington is a small town nestled between the Blackdown Hills and the Quantock Hills. It is primarily a commuter town, most of its working-age population employed in neighbouring Taunton or in the agricultural industry. The wool trade is the traditional source of wealth in the town and until the early 20th Century, one of the largest traders in the area was the Fox family. Their business diversified locally, and they even set up their own bank in the late 18th Century. Fox, Fowler and Company was an independent bank that was the last to hold the legal rights to print its own notes. That right was lost when Fox, Fowler and Company was taken over by Lloyds Bank in 1921. Since then, only the Bank of England retains the right to print currency in England. Banks in Scotland and Northern Ireland do have consent to print sterling notes. There are said to be two Fox Fowler notes in circulation.

The Blackdown Hills line the border between Somerset and Devon. Wellington and Taunton abutting the northern slopes, the Devon towns of Honiton and Axminster abutting the southern slopes. The River Axe flows alongside the southeastern slopes of the Blackdown Hills and lends its name to the Devon town of Axminster. Historically a carpet manufacturing town, a type of weaving was invented in the town that is now used by carpet weavers all over the world. There is a link via the M5 to Kidderminster, the main British town to produce 'Axminster Carpets' on an industrial scale. Only cattle that graze in the Axe Valley produce the milk required for Devonshire Clotted Cream.

Tarka Trail

Junction 27: The A361, Exmoor, Barnstaple and the Atlantic Coast

The A38 joins the M5 once again at Junction 27 and continues to run south concurrently with the motorway until it re-emerges at the M5's southern terminus below Exeter. The original route of the A38 between Junctions 27 and 31 was downgraded to become the B3181 after the opening of this final stretch of the M5 in 1975. As a result, the B3181 can quickly build up with traffic should there be any incidents on this stretch of motorway.

The A361 heads west of Junction 27, taking motorists towards Ilfracombe and connecting with the A39 Atlantic Highway at Barnstaple. Despite several gaps in the route, the A361 is 195 miles in length and has the distinction of being the longest three-digit A-class road in Britain. Its northern terminus is outside Rugby in Warwickshire. The final section between Junction 27 and Ilfracombe is a beautiful road to drive on, especially on a clear day.

The first town that motorists pass is Tiverton, a pleasant market town aside the River Exe. Since the M5 opened in the mid-1970s, Tiverton has evolved into a dormitory town for people who work in Taunton or Exeter, but its traditional trade was wool. The town owes its historic growth to wealthy wool merchants over the centuries, one of whom was Peter Blundell, founder of the famous Blundell's School. Tiverton Castle was built overlooking the River Exe during the 12th Century but this was dismantled during the English Civil War. The following century, a residence was built for a wealthy local family: the Wests.

The A361 entirely bypasses Tiverton and crosses the River Exe. It then heads due northwest towards Barnstaple. Looking north from it, panoramic views of Exmoor can be enjoyed. The second of the National Parks, Exmoor is roughly coterminous with a former Royal Hunting Ground established by the Prince Regent in 1818. More than two thirds of it are in Somerset, the remainder being in Devon. Its highest point is Dunkery Beacon at 1,705ft above sea level. The National Park includes 34 miles of coastline, also featuring the highest sea cliff on mainland Britain: Great Hangman outside Coombe Martin is 1,043 feet high.

Barnstaple is an important town for the North Devon area. Situated on the estuary of the River Taw, it is a crossroads for the A39 and A361. There is a large pannier market in the town that is open Monday-Saturday but has a different set of traders on each day. It is an attractive purpose-built structure that was completed in 1856.

The town is also now the terminus for the branch line from Exeter known as the Tarka Line. Before the Beaching Report in the early 1960s, the Tarka Line used to continue beyond Bideford to Great Torrington. The 9-mile section between Barnstaple and Bideford is now a very popular walking and cycling route, the Tarka Trail. It was 'reopened' as a railway briefly in 2011, but in 00 gauge by television presenter, James May, who raced his Hornby model of the Flying Scotsman against a locomotive owned by German model railway enthusiasts.

The River Taw flows into the western extreme of the Bristol Channel and shares its estuary with the River Torridge flowing from the south. The Bristol Channel extends only another ten miles west to Hartland Point, at which stage sailors will be on the Atlantic Ocean. The Royal Marines have several facilities on the estuaries of both the Taw and the Torridge. Their fast attack boats and helicopters can often be seen on training exercises in the area.

After Barnstaple, motorists can either follow the A361 towards the coastal towns of Woolacombe and Ilfracombe or the A39, continuing swiftly into Bideford and Westward Ho! The latter having the distinction of being the only place name in Britain to contain an exclamation mark. It then follows the Atlantic Coast of Cornwall, connecting to fabulous towns and villages such as Bude, Boscastle and Padstow before cutting across the Cornish Peninsula to the south coast, culminating at Falmouth.

Junction 28: Cullompton & Honiton

Cullompton is a small town. Like its near neighbour Tiverton, it was traditionally a centre for trading wool but it evolved over time to leather making. It is now primarily a dormitory town for Exeter. The farmers market occurs only once per month, but it is the oldest in the southwest, dating back to 1278. Following the Beaching Report, Cullompton was deprived of its railway station. However, the Bristol–Exeter Railway line runs between Junction 28 and the town and it runs parallel with the motorway for around twenty miles, between Wellington and the village of Hele. A unique attraction a few miles north of Cullompton is Diggerland, which can be seen aside the M5. It provides a variety of tractors and heavy machinery that members of the family, young and old, can enjoy playing with. It can be accessed via the B3181.

As the crow flies, Junction 28 is the closest to Honiton by using the A373. The town is known for its tradition of lacemaking. Queen Victoria's wedding dress was made of Honiton Lace although the dress was sewn together in the coastal village of Beer. Honiton is situated on the route of the Fosse Way, running southwest-northeast across the Blackdown Hills. As such the town was a stopping point for Roman legions travelling the last or first leg of the road to or from Exeter.

Parliament Street, Exeter

Junction 29: The Fosse Way, the A30 and Exeter

At Junction 29, the M5 crosses the A30, a road that is doubly significant. It is over two millennia old, marking the first stage of the Fosse Way out of Exeter. As mentioned in the section about Junction 11A and Cirencester, the Fosse Way cuts across England from the south west to the north east, connecting Exeter and Lincoln. 230 miles in length, it is almost a perfect straight line – never veering more than six miles from a direct line between the two cities.

The other significance of this stretch of road is that it is now designated as the A30, a major trunk road connecting the West London Borough of

Hounslow with Land's End. It is a continuous road stretching 284 miles but large sections of it have been made redundant as a primary route by the dualling of the A303 and opening of the M3. West of Exeter, however, it is arguably the most important road in and out of Cornwall, being continuous dual carriageway from Exeter through to Carland Cross, six miles to the north of the city of Truro. Like the A38 from Junction 27, the A30 runs concurrently with the M5 from Junction 29 to Junction 31 where it heads towards Okehampton and into Cornwall.

Less than half a mile from Junction 29 is the Headquarters of the Meteorological Office, more commonly known as the Met Office. Part of the British Government's Department for Business, Energy and Industrial Strategy, it collects atmospheric, weather and climate data and uses it to predict the short-term weather and long-term climate. It was initially set up as a trading arm of the Ministry of Defence but has been within the remit of various Government Departments that deal with the Environment since 1990. The names of Government Departments change due to mergers and splits every few years so it is likely the Department for Business, Energy and Industrial Strategy may change its name again. The Met Office provides weather forecast information for a number of media outlets, the most notable being ITV. The BBC has used weather forecast information from a different provider, the Dutch MeteoGroup, since 2015. However, the Shipping Forecast broadcast daily on Radio 4 is provided by the Met Office. Weather warnings, particularly those with severe consequences such as the probability of snow, strong winds, risk of flooding etc., are issued by the Met Office and are still announced by the BBC's news outlets.

Exeter's Roman past is mostly hidden and has been uncovered over time by excavations. Aside from the Cathedral and a handful of other exceptions, Exeter's centre has been mostly constructed since the end of the Second World War. It was the target of the 'Baedeker Blitz', a German air offensive intended to destroy cities and towns of high cultural and historic value. Baedeker Travel Guides are very popular to this day and provide inspiration to many a traveller. The most recent development for Exeter's centre is the Princesshay Shopping Centre, which is sympathetically built around the remains of the 15th Century St Catherine's Chapel and its Alms Houses.

The Centre of Exeter and the Docks are well worth exploring. Parliament Street, joined with High Street, is one of the narrowest 'streets' in the world. It is 2ft 1in wide at its narrowest and 4ft wide at its broadest. The overall length is 160ft. A detour down West Street is worthwhile to see 'the house that moved'. In 1961, the 14th Century property was moved in its entirety over 100 yards from its original position to make way for the city's ring road. Weighing 21 tonnes, it was strapped up and moved only inches at a time to preserve one of the few historic buildings in the city.

A fifteen-minute walk from the Cathedral takes visitors to Exeter Quayside, another regenerated part of the city centre that provides a more continental atmosphere with waterside cafes and bars. Freight vessels no longer use the canal to sail into Exeter and so the water is entirely used for leisure. Canoes can be rented at the Quayside. Pedestrians can cross the River Exe towards the Quayside via the Butts Ferry, a cable operated service that has been in service 1641. The city's oldest brick-built structure, the Customs House, is nearby. It was constructed in 1680 and can be visited as part of the city's guided tours organised by the Tourist Information centre.

Exeter City Football Club play in the fourth tier of English League football, they have never played above the third tier. They play their home games at St James's Park, a ground that shares its name with the home stadium of Newcastle United. Famous fans of Exeter City include Coldplay frontman, Chris Martin and television personalities Noel Edmonds and Adrian Edmondson. Spoon-bending magician Uri Geller was a previous director on the club's board and once famously hosted a visit of popstar, Michael Jackson, to St James's Park. Exeter's more popular sport is rugby. Exeter Chiefs were founded in 1871 and play their home games at Sandy Park. They are the only club to be champions of all of the top four tiers of English rugby.

Sidmouth viewed from Connaught Gardens

Junction 30: Topsham, Exmouth & the East Devon Coast

Towering above Junction 30 is Sandy Park, home of Exeter's Rugby Club, Exeter Chiefs. As well as serving the city of Exeter, Junction 30 is the primary exit for destinations in East Devon. From here, the A3052 heads east and passes through or near to Sidmouth, Seaton, Axmouth and then continues into Dorset, culminating between Lyme Regis and Charmouth. It is also a very scenic road and it leads to some of the finest places along the south coast of England.

Less than a mile from Junction 30 is the village Clyst St Mary, situated aside the River Clyst that lends its name to several settlements on its course. In 1549 it was the scene of one of many battles in the West Country that formed the Prayer Book Rebellion, a Catholic resistance against Edward VI. After the Battle of Clyst St Mary, 900 of the Catholic rebels who had been arrested were executed on nearby Clyst Heath.

At Clyst St Mary, motorists can either turn south on the A376 towards Exmouth or continue along the A3052. The A376 passes the turning for Topsham, a small town on the Exe estuary founded by the Romans as a port. Modern Topsham is a quiet town and the former warehouse on the quayside is now an antiques and collectables centre that spans three storeys, a must-see for collectors. The Exmouth branch line runs parallel to the A376. It is informally known as the Avocet Line as the birds are known to nest on the Exe estuary. One of the stations, Lympstone, serves the primary training centre for the Royal Marines.

Exmouth is one of the oldest established seaside resorts in England. During the late 18th and early 19th Centuries, it benefited from investment from the wealthiest in society who were cut off from their usual holiday destinations on continental Europe during the Napoleonic wars. Three decades later Exmouth benefited further with the advent of the railways. It has a modest harbour that was a regular terminal for Sir Walter Raleigh, who was born in a village nearby. A connection to another Maritime Hero is Lady Nelson, the estranged wife of Admiral Lord Nelson, who is buried in the churchyard at Littleham. A seasonal passenger ferry operates between Exmouth and Starcross on the west banks of the Exe estuary.

Heading east from Clyst St Mary, the A3052 abuts the northern edge of Woodbury Common, a mass of open land that is frequented by walkers, cyclists and grazing farm animals. It is also used for non-combat training exercises by the Royal Marines based at nearby Lympstone. Part of Woodbury Common is a Golf Course that is owned by former Racing Driver, Nigel Mansell. One of his Formula One cars used to be on display in the foyer of the clubhouse.

Another mile after Clyst St Mary is the interestingly named village of Cat & Fiddle. It is named after the public house with a holiday home park behind it. Over time, the owners of the holiday homes have become permanent residents and so it has become a community. Another couple of miles further east, the A3052 is crossed by the B3180 at a staggered crossroads. Immediately after the crossroads there is an Automobile Association (AA) Box, numbered 456. This is a rare sight as very few remain in their original positions. Long standing members of the AA may still have a key to access the box to make a phone call for assistance.

The B3180 northbound will take motorists to Ottery St Mary, a small town in the Otter Valley that was the birthplace of the poet, Samuel Taylor Coleridge. Legend has it that the town was previously blighted by pixies, who were eventually banished when the bells of the Parish Church were installed. Turning south on the B3180 will take motorists through the centre of Woodbury Common towards Exmouth or Budleigh Salterton. After the staggered crossroads, the A3052 then continues and descends into the Otter Valley, through the village of Newton Poppleford. Upon entering the village, motorists are greeted by charming wooden sculptures of a family of bears that are out fishing aside a brook. At the far end of the village, the road crosses the River Otter and then ascends quickly uphill.

The next descent of the A3052 takes motorists into the Sid Valley, the main settlement of which is Sidmouth. Nestled between red cliffs and boasting fine regency architecture, visitors will have a hard time trying to name more a picturesque town on the south coast of England. On clear days, views can be enjoyed as far east as Portland, and as far west as Torbay. Hotels in the town are of the highest quality and are frequented by repeat visitors. The retail centre is large for a town of its size but this only compliments Sidmouth as it is dominated by independent traders. Connaught Gardens is a fine open space overlooking the town and features a rapid descent to the beach via Jacob's Ladder.

At Sidford, the A3052 is connected to the A375, a narrow and twisting A-Class road that heads north towards Honiton eventually overlooking the Otter Valley. It passes through the village of Sidbury where St Giles's Church has a bunker beneath it. This was used to store gunpowder in preparation for a possible invasion of Britain during the Napoleonic Wars.

The fishing village of Beer cannot be seen from the A3052 as it is sheltered by the gorge in which it lies. It is the westernmost point on the south coast with limestone cliffs. There are several manmade caves around Beer, the limestone having been quarried and used for many construction projects across the country. It has been exported overseas. 24 British cathedrals, Christchurch in New Zealand and St Louis, Missouri, have used Beer stone due to its ease for carving.

The next town is Seaton. If motorists enter Seaton via the B3174 they are greeted with an incredible view across the town and the Estuary of the River Axe. As a retail centre, Seaton is somewhat limited however the seafront has a unique phenomenon, with a section of red cliffs sandwiched between limestone cliffs. The former railway branch line that served the town until 1966 has since been converted into a tramway. The tram station in Seaton was rebuilt in the late 2010s and now features a museum and café.

After Seaton, the A3052 then continues into the neighbouring county of Dorset and the historic town of Lyme Regis. The Royal suffix was given to Lyme Regis by Edward 1 as it was one of his naval bases. The Cobb, an ancient harbour wall, extends into the English Channel and until the early 19th Century it was one of the busiest ports in England. More so than the likes of Liverpool and Bristol. Eventually Lyme Regis's influence as a port waned as the size of trading vessels grew.

Babbacombe Model Village

Approaching Junction 31: The end of the motorway but not the end of the journey

After Junction 30, the M5 crosses the River Exe and the Exeter Ship Canal in quick succession. Looking northwest, motorists may see the weir that was built by the Countess of Devon during the 13th Century to power her mills. This caused angst amongst ocean-going traders as they were cut off from Exeter's docks and forced to offload their cargo at Topsham, where they would be charged significant tolls to transport their goods across land.

The discovery of North America and Elizabeth I's non-confrontational foreign policy gave England a boom in overseas trading. The requirement for a more direct route from Exeter to the open sea was required. By the 1560s, construction began on the Exeter Ship Canal, a route that would bypass the weir constructed by the Countess of Devon three centuries previously. This gave rise to the Quayside in the centre of Exeter.

When crossing the Exe and the canal, motorists can view Exmouth Harbour and the Dawlish Warren peninsula if they look southeast. Once over the waterways, the M5 terminates just over a mile further west. At this point motorists have three options at the Junction 31 interchange: join the A30 to continue towards Cornwall or continue along the A38 towards Plymouth. Another couple of miles later, motorists can join the A380 towards Torbay.

The first couple of miles of the A30 past Junction 31 offer panoramic views of Exeter from the south, including the Cathedral elevated above the Quayside. The A38 and the A380 both climb Telegraph Hill, a name that was given to the northern slope of the Haldon Hills in the early 20th Century. It was the site of a transmitter for relaying communications between Britain's warships and the Admiralty. The interchange between the A38 and A380 is an accident blackspot in both directions, partly due to the steep gradient on this section of dual carriageway.

Motorists heading to Torbay on the A380 can now enjoy an uninterrupted journey to the outskirts of Torquay, the entire route was upgraded to a dual carriageway in 2018. It crosses the River Teign and provides a useful link to Teignmouth, a must visit place for rail enthusiasts. Isambard Kingdom Brunel's Exeter-Plymouth line runs at the foot the red cliffs, yet only a few feet from the waves of the English Channel. Another example of British engineering from the 1840s made even more marvellous by the fact it is relied on nearly two centuries later. The A380 then bypasses Newton Abbott, home of Britain's most westerly racecourse.

Torquay, Paignton and Brixham make up Torbay. Along with Exmouth, it is one of the oldest holiday resorts in Britain. Its beginnings as a holiday destination stem from the Napoleonic Wars. British warships would shelter in Torbay and the natural beauty of the area would pique the interest of wealthy naval officers. Indeed, those that had served in the Mediterranean compared Torbay favourably with the French Riviera. A replica of Sir Francis Drake's ship, the Golden Hinde, can be found in Brixham harbour. Also, a brilliant model village in nearby Babbacombe is well worth the diversion and it is illuminated on Thursday evenings.

At the top of Telegraph Hill, the A38 passes Exeter Racecourse. It is continuous dual carriageway to the city of Plymouth but this narrows to single carriageway at the Tamar Bridge. There are further brief stretches of dual carriageway between Saltash and the end of the A38 at Bodmin. From there, motorists can then use the A30 to continue to England's most westerly point at Land's End.

The River Tamar forms the boundary between Devon and Cornwall. There are only three miles between the north coast of Cornwall and the source of the River Tamar, almost making Cornwall an island. The Tamar Bridge is a suspension bridge that opened in 1961 but underwent widening and partial reconstruction forty years later. Undeniably the most impressive feature of the Tamar crossing is the Royal Albert Bridge. Another impressive design from Isambard Kingdom Brunel, carrying the Plymouth–Penzance railway line into Cornwall since 1859. Since the late 1960s, this has been the only railway line into Cornwall.

The Royal Albert Bridge crossing the River Tamar

Lightning Source UK Ltd.
Milton Keynes UK
UKHW051045260922
409449UK00006B/84